# MINISTERING THROUGH
# SPIRITUAL GIFTS

# CHARLES
# STANLEY

OLIVER
NELSON

THOMAS NELSON PUBLISHERS
Nashville

Published in Nashville, Tennessee, by Thomas Nelson, Inc.

The Bible version used in this publication is THE NEW KING JAMES VERSION. Copyright © 1979, 1980, 1982, Thomas Nelson, Inc., Publishers.

ISBN 0-7852-7287-9

Printed in the United States of America
12 PHX 04 03

# Contents

# GOD'S SPECIAL GIFT TO YOU

D o you know your innate spiritual gift? Have you identified the most important gift that God has given to you for the purposes of ministry in His name?

Every person has been given a spiritual gift from God—a gift designed to be used as part of the body of Christ and for the purpose of assisting others. These gifts reside in a person from the time the person accepts Jesus Christ as his personal Savior. They are intended to be the main avenue through which a person ministers to others within the church as a whole.

These gifts are ones that I and others call "motivational gifts," for these are the gifts residing in us to *motivate* us toward service. They are gifts that compel, cause, and inspire us to act in specific ways. They are the particular bent we have to serve God's people and others whom we desire to see become Christians.

I believe it is vitally important to our personal spiritual lives, as well as to the overall spiritual life of a church, for us to recognize these gifts, to encourage their proper use in the church, and to encourage one another as we exercise our gifts.

## The Nature of Motivational Gifts

Several things about these gifts are vital for us to acknowledge at the outset of our study:

1. *Every person has received a "motivational" gift.* Some people may seem gifted with a number of them, but one of the seven gifts covered in this study is going to be dominant in a person's life. The gift is resident from a person's birth, and it becomes fully operative for its God-given purposes when a person is born again.

2. *The motivational gifts are intended to be used in the church for the spiritual edification or building up of God's people.* Each of the motivational gifts covered in this study *may* be employed "in the flesh." When this happens, disaster generally follows. The misuse of the gifts is actually counterproductive to the work that the Holy Spirit desires to do in us individually and in the church as a whole. We must rely completely upon the Holy Spirit to assist us in the use of our motivational gifts.

3. *We are commanded by God to use these gifts.* Peter wrote to the church, "As each one has received a gift, minister it to one another, as good stewards of the manifold grace of God" (1 Peter 4:10).

4. *The motivational gifts are* resident *in the believer.* These gifts are built into a person's personality. They are "who" we are in the church. Other gifts are identified in the New Testament as being gifts that are resident in the Holy Spirit—such gifts operate "as the Spirit wills" and may be manifested in any believer's life from time to time and in various situations. (See 1 Cor. 12:4–6 for such a list.) The motivational gifts, however, do not come and go in the believer's life. They are permanent. For example, a person does not manifest the motivational gift of prophecy for six months, and then shift to a motivational gift of service for the next three years, and then shift to another gift. Motivational gifts span the course of a person's life, and although they may manifest in slightly different ways, in different situations, with varying degrees of intensity, the *identity* of the gift remains intact and is unchangeable.

5. *We each have a responsibility to discover and then to use our spiritual gifts.* The more we learn about our spiritual gifts, the greater the responsibility we have to use them for the benefit

of others. The first thing we each must recognize is that we *have* a motivational gift given to us by God; then we must recognize which of the seven gifts have been given. That is a major step for many believers who have never considered themselves to be "gifted" by God in any particular way. Let me repeat again: *you* have been given a spiritual motivational gift by God. *You* bear this as part of your identity. *You* are responsible for identifying your gift, developing it, and then using it for the glory of God. The more you use your motivational gift, the more you will grow in it, and the more the Holy Spirit will be able to use you in it.

## No Spectators Allowed

The church was never designed by God to include spectators. Every person within the church—which is the greater Body of Christ—was and is expected to be vibrantly alive and active, each one using his resident motivational gift at all times and in as many situations as possible, and each believer being open to use by the Holy Spirit "as the Spirit wills" in the manifestation of other spiritual gifts.

So many people in the church today are sitting on the sidelines watching others take active roles. Some have estimated that eighty percent of those who attend a church regularly "watch" the other twenty percent do the work of the church. That is detrimental to the individuals who are inactive, to the individuals who are active, and to the work of the Lord as a whole. It certainly is not God's desire or design.

God desires that each person be active in the use of his gifts so that the following might occur:

- Each person may grow more and more into the fullness of what God intended in their lives from the moment of their creation
- The work within the church may be evenly distributed so that nobody reaches the state of overload or burn out

• The work of the church as a whole may be effective, vibrant, and balanced.

This study is designed to help you understand the spiritual gifts, but even more so, it is intended to help you identify *your* particular gift and to motivate you toward the use of that gift.

I believe two things will happen as you truly understand who you are in Christ Jesus—and what your identity is within the Body of Christ. First, I believe you are going to be excited about your identity and the ways in which God desires to use you. Second, I believe you are going to be challenged to develop your gift and employ it to the best of your ability.

God has many special rewards reserved for those who employ their motivational ministry gifts to the best of their abilities—don't miss out on them!

# LESSON 1

# APPROACHING THE MOTIVATIONAL GIFTS

A number of books are available today that help a person understand their individual talents and abilities and learn more about how to use them to achieve success. This book is unlike them in two ways:

First, this book is intended for Bible study. It is not a stand-alone book. I hope you will refer to your Bible again and again, and that you will mark specific words, underline phrases, or write in the margins of your personal Bible.

Second, this book is intended to help you discover the *spiritual* gift that God has given to you and built into your very personality, so that you will use this gift—not for your own personal success—but for the success of the Body of Christ as a whole. Certainly, each of us benefits and grows spiritually when we employ our spiritual motivational gifts. Certainly, God rewards us for using these gifts in the proper way. However, the intent for using the spiritual gifts is not personal gain, but the building up of others within the church.

Because these gifts are spiritual in nature, they are not going to be readily understood by those who do not have a personal relationship with Jesus Christ. All of what we come to understand about our spiritual motivational gifts and their use is revealed to us by the Holy Spirit. Therefore, this study should be undertaken by those who are believers in Christ Jesus and who desire both to know and to use their gifts effectively.

In our study we will use the terms "ministry gifts" and "motivational gifts" interchangeably. They are spiritual gifts that motivate us to minister to others. They are ministry gifts in that they are always intended to build up others in the Body of Christ.

# Keys to Study

You will be asked in this study to respond to the material that is presented in one of the following ways:

- What new insight have you gained?
- Have you ever had a similar experience?
- How do you feel about this?
- In what way are you challenged to act?

## Insights

A spiritual insight may be likened to a new degree of understanding. It lies beyond a literal understanding of a fact or a concept. Rather, it involves an understanding of God's *meaning* and His *purposes*.

Spiritual insights come to us as we read, study, and meditate on the Bible. Very often they come to us almost as a surprise. We may have read a passage numerous times, but then God reveals new meaning to us.

Insights are usually very personal—most of them involve some way in which the passage has meaning to your past or present life experiences.

Spiritual insights are the direct work of the Holy Spirit in our lives as we read God's Word. They are a part of the Holy Spirit's function as the Spirit of truth—it is the Spirit who reveals to us precisely what is important for us to know or learn at any given moment in our lives so that we might grow in Christ and respond to specific situations and circumstances with godly decisions and behavior.

Ask the Holy Spirit to give you insights every time you open your Bible to read and study it. I believe God delights in answering such a prayer. In fact, if you haven't gained a new spiritual insight after reading several passages from God's Word, you likely haven't been engaged in the process of genuine study. The person who truly studies God's Word with an open heart and an eagerness to hear from the Holy Spirit is going to enjoy spiritual insights on a regular basis.

Make notes about your spiritual insights. This practice will benefit you in two ways. First, as you look back in the margins of your Bible and read what God has shown you or spoken to you in the past, and then reflect on how that insight manifests itself in the subsequent months or years of your life, your faith will grow. Second, making notes of spiritual insights is a way of being more intentional as you read God's Word. The more we are looking for spiritual insights, the more often we seem to grasp them.

## Experiences

We each come to God's Word with a different set of life experiences, which operate as something of a filter through which we understand the Bible's content. Each individual therefore has a slightly different perspective on any scriptural passage. In a group setting, these differences can sometimes create problems. This is especially true as we are studying spiritual motivation gifts. For example, the person who is gifted in prophecy is going to see the world in a particular way and is going to have experiences related to the manifestation of the gift of prophecy in and through his life. The person who is gifted in service is going to see the world in a much different way and is going to have experiences related to the operation of that particular gift. The two sets of experiences may be very different in nature, and these differences impact the meaning that a person draws from a particular passage of Scripture.

We must be very cautious in this study to allow for these differences. The differences do not weaken us as a body of believers, rather they strengthen us. Do not let your experiential differences divide you as a group. Recognize that various motivational gifts are at work *in the interpretation of the various passages you will be studying.*

Many of our life experiences are ones we hold in common. Furthermore, we each can point to times in which we have discovered the truth of a Bible passage to be highly relevant to our lives. We can recall times when the Bible confirmed, encouraged, convicted, challenged, or directed us in some way. Be willing to explore these times and to share them with others.

Our experiences do not make the Bible true. The Bible is truth, period. The value in sharing experiences is this: we see more clearly and more broadly how the truth of God's Word is *applied* to us as individuals. We have a growing understanding that God's Word is true for all people of all ages in all cultures throughout history. We see how God's Word relates to us as a whole, and also to us as individuals. No other book is like the Bible in its ability to speak to each person individually and personally, and yet to speak to the whole of the church collectively.

Sharing experiences is important for your spiritual growth. It is a part of your witness for Christ Jesus. Not only will you benefit from hearing the experiences of others, but you will benefit from sharing your own experiences. You will become more skilled at communicating your faith and in talking about spiritual matters. Those of you who are doing this as an individual study should find avenues for sharing your faith-related experiences with others. Those of you who will be sharing in a small-group setting should be open to hearing what others say so that you can learn, adapt, and apply God's Word more diligently to your own life. Be cautious on this point: keep your discussion of experiences focused on the Scriptures. Do not simply talk about experiences for the sake of calling attention to the experience. Make sure your experiences are directly related to the passages of Scripture being studied.

A tendency arises when we share experiences to judge the experiences of others. Avoid that tendency! A judgmental attitude—especially toward a person's motivational ministry gifts—can result in great harm. Others will sense your judgmental spirit, and you will open the door to division and friction in the group. Listen. Discuss. Talk about what the Scriptures say and mean. But be careful not to judge or to condemn others, even in the spirit of so-called "poking innocent fun" at yourself or another person.

## Emotional Response

Just as we each have unique life experiences and a unique perspective on the Scriptures, we each have our own emotional responses to God's Word. No emotional response is more valid than another. In many ways, our emotional response to the Bible is closely linked with our spiritual motivational gift. The person who is gifted in exhortation, for example, may approach a particular passage in the Bible with a very different set of emotions than a person who has been given the motivational gift of mercy.

As you allow for different perspectives and life experiences, allow for different emotional responses. Face your emotions honestly, and allow others the freedom to share their emotions fully. Every emotion is valid.

Again, our emotions do not give validity to the Scriptures, and our emotions should never be used as a gauge of faith. Our faith is always to be based on what God says, not on what we feel. The Scriptures are true regardless of the emotions they evoke in us. At the same time, we must recognize that the Bible has an emotional impact on us. We cannot read the Bible with an open heart and mind and not have an emotional response to it. To do so would be to deny a part of our basic personality and spiritual identity.

Few fields of study are more laden with emotion than a study of the motivational gifts. These gifts play a part in who we *are* in our personalities and in our identities. We each have very strong and deep-seated feelings about God and His Word based upon the spiritual gift we have been given. As you share your opinions and others share theirs, recognize that God has given us our emotions and we each must learn to control our emotions, to use them wisely, and to appreciate the emotional responses of others as valid.

Bible study groups can become sidetracked by opinions that lead to debate, distrust, and confusion. Focus your group sharing on feelings and experiences, not opinions. Allow others to draw their own conclusions directly from God's Word, without the influence of a strongly held personal opinion.

Because spiritual gifts are intensely personal and we each feel a certain degree of "ownership" of our gifts, avoid the tendency to become defensive about your own gift. Seek instead to discover ways in which you might use your gift more effectively and to employ it in a more loving manner. The one emotion that is central to the use of all the motivational gifts is love.

## Challenges

As we read the Bible, we often come to verses that seem to speak directly to us. Something challenges us to change an aspect of our lives or to take a specific action. We may feel conviction of sin. We may feel the need to correct something in the way we think, speak, or act toward others. We may feel compelled to seek forgiveness of a person or to change our attitude or understanding about another person's actions. As I read the Scriptures and pray, or talk about the Scriptures with other people and pray with them, I often feel those challenges to grow and extend myself. I believe it is vitally important, therefore, for each of us to be aware of the ways in which God may speak to us through His Word to challenge us, stretch us, change us, or cause our faith to grow. *Expect* to be challenged!

God desires that we function as a "body"—each person contributing his or her gifts for the healing, enrichment, and edification of the whole body. We are *challenged* to do this in God's Word, and the individual challenges we feel regarding the development of our personal gift should always be seen in the light of this greater challenge. The challenge of God's Word to us will always be that we recognize our gift, develop our gift, and use our gift *as the Holy Spirit leads and guides us on a daily basis.* We must be open continually to the ways in which the Holy Spirit will teach us and direct our paths.

God's ultimate reason for us to know His Word is so that we might live out His Word in our daily lives, and in so doing, to share His Word with others. We are to be His witnesses and to carry on the mission of Jesus Christ to the world. We are never to be hearers of the Word only—but *doers* of the Word (see James 1:22). Perhaps in no other Christian action is this more evident that in the use of our spiritual motivational gifts. God expects us to *employ* our gifts and to become skilled and experienced in the use of our gifts.

As you discuss spiritual gifts in a small-group setting, look for those in your group who may have your same gift. If you have had more experience in developing your motivational gift, you may want to seek ways to have a closer relationship with others who share the same gift so that you can help them grow in the use of their gift. If you are newly recognizing your motivational gift, you may want to have a mentoring relationship with others who have more experience in using the gift. We each will find ourselves in a position of giving/sharing or receiving/learning as this study unfolds. Much benefit is derived from recognizing the diversity of our gifts, but much benefit can also be derived from forming relationships with those who share our same gift.

We are to grow in the use of our spiritual gifts all our lives. Your development of your motivational gift will not end with the conclusion of this ten-lesson study. It is a lifelong quest. Continue to allow others to minister to you through their gifts, and continue to find ways to minister to others through your gifts. Be open always to the Holy Spirit's guidance.

## Personal or Group Study

This book has been designed for small-group study. If you do not have someone with whom you can share your insights, experiences, emotions, and challenges, I encourage you to find someone. Perhaps you can start a Bible study in your home. Perhaps you can talk to your pastor about organizing a Bible study group in your church. There is much to be learned on your own. There is much more to be learned in a small-group setting.

If you are using this book for personal study, I encourage you to share with a spouse, child, or close friend some of the insights you gain about motivational gifts.

## Keep the Bible Central

A tendency of a group devoted to a study of motivational gifts is for the group to enter into discussions that are not focused on the Bible. Keep the Bible at the center of all you do and discuss. I encourage you to gather around God's Word as if you were gathering around a banquet table for a spiritually nutritious meal—one with a diversity of foods so that all the nutrients each person needs are available. Remember, your time together should be spent in a *study* of the Bible. Allow the Bible to feed you and to become life to you.

## Prayer

As you begin each lesson, ask God to give you spiritual eyes to see what He wants you to see and spiritual ears to hear what He wants you to hear. Ask Him to give you new insights, to recall experiences that relate to what you read, and to help you identify your emotions clearly. Ask Him to reveal to you what He desires for you to be, say, and do.

As you conclude your time of study, ask the Lord to seal what you have learned in your heart so you will never forget it. Ask Him to transform you more into the likeness of Jesus Christ as you meditate on what you have studied. Above all, ask Him to give you the courage to become, say, and do what He has challenged you to become, say, and do.

As you pray, be keenly aware that God desires to impart to you His truth about your particular spiritual gift, as well as truth about all other motivational gifts. Be sensitive to what He may reveal to you or speak to you as you pray about your particular gift.

Consider these questions as you begin your study:

- *What new insights do you hope to gain about your own spiritual motivational gift?*

_____

_____

- *What insights do you hope to gain about how the motivational gifts are intended to function in the church as a whole?*

_____

_____

- *Do you know your motivational gift, and have you had experience developing it?*

_____

_____

- *In what areas have you struggled in the past regarding your motivational gift or the motivational gifts of others?*

_____

_____

• *How do you feel about the fact that God has given to each person a spiritual motivational gift?*

_____

_____

• *Are you open to being challenged to develop your motivational gift and to use it more openly within the Body of Christ?*

_____

_____

# LESSON 2

# AN OVERVIEW OF THE MINISTRY GIFTS

The motivational gifts were identified by the apostle Paul in his letter to the Romans. He prefaced his definition of the seven motivational gifts, however, with an admonition that is vital for us to remember always as we engage in this study: "For as we have many members in one body, but all the members do not have the same function, so we, being many, are one body in Christ, and individually members of one another" (Rom. 12:4–5).

At the very outset of our study of the motivational gifts I want you to focus on Paul's statement that "all the members do not have the same function" and yet all are "one body in Christ." We can be different, and yet be united! We have different gifts and roles to play within the church, and yet there are many things that we share in common. As concerned as Paul was about our individual gifts, he was equally concerned that the church regard itself as a whole and function as a whole.

• *Recall a situation or instance in your life in which diversity and unity were both present.*

_____

_____

## What the Word Says

For we, though many, are one bread and one body; for we all partake of that one bread.
(1 Cor. 10:17)

You are all one in Christ Jesus.
(Gal 3:28)

There is one body and one Spirit, just as you were called in one hope of your calling; one Lord, one faith, one baptism; one God and Father of all, who is above all, and through all, and in you all.
(Eph. 4:4–6)

## What the Word Says to Me

-----------------------------

-----------------------------

-----------------------------

-----------------------------

-----------------------------

-----------------------------

-----------------------------

-----------------------------

-----------------------------

-----------------------------

-----------------------------

-----------------------------

-----------------------------

The apostle Paul also wrote about our diversity and unity to the Corinthians:

There are diversities of gifts, but the same Spirit. There are differences of ministries, but the same Lord. And there are diversities of activities, but it is the same God who works all in all. But the manifestation of the Spirit is given to each one for the profit of all . . . For as the body is one and has many members, but all the members of that one body, being many, are one body, so also is Christ. For by one Spirit we were all baptized into one body—whether Jews or Greeks, whether slaves or free— ·

and have all been made to drink into one Spirit. For in fact the body is not one member but many.

If the foot should say, "Because I am not a hand, I am not of the body," is it therefore not of the body? And if the ear should say, "Because I am not an eye, I am not of the body," is it therefore not of the body? If the whole body were an eye, where would be the hearing? If the whole were hearing, where would be the smelling? But now God has set the members, each one of them, in the body just as He pleased. And if they were all one member, where would the body be . . .

But God composed the body, having given greater honor to that part which lacks it, that there should be no schism in the body, but that the members should have the same care for one another. And if one member suffers, all the members suffer with it; or if one member is honored, all the members rejoice with it. (1 Cor. 12:4–7, 12–19, 24–26)

- *What new insights do you have into this passage of Scripture?*

_____

_____

- *In your experience, what happens when a group becomes divided by the pride of some members?*

_____

_____

## Seven Gifts Given for Ministry Purposes

It is against the backdrop of a unified body that the apostle Paul identified seven motivational gifts:

Having then gifts differing according to the grace that is given to us, let us use them: if prophecy, let us prophesy

in proportion to our faith; or ministry, let us use it in
our ministering; he who teaches, in teaching; he who
exhorts, in exhortation; he who gives, with liberality; he
who leads, with diligence; he who shows mercy, with
cheerfulness. (Rom. 12:6–8)

Note clearly the seven gifts that Paul identifies:

1. prophecy
2. ministering, which may also be called service
3. teaching
4. exhortation
5. giving
6. leading, which may also be called administration or organization
7. mercy

Paul further states in this passage that each person has one
of these gifts resident in himself or herself "according to the
grace that has been given to us" (v. 5). God is the giver of the
gifts, and through His Holy Spirit He is the one who helps us
identify, develop, and use our gifts. These are not gifts that we
"work up" or that we have the privilege to choose for ourselves.
They are a gift of God to us. We must recognize how we are
made, embrace our own gift, and then seek to grow in it.

Below are seven verses that relate to each of these seven
motivational gifts. Many verses relate to each gift, but these
verses are offered here as an overview introduction. As you
read through these gifts, recognize that motivational gifts are
to be used in all contexts of our life: at home, in one-on-one
encounters, and on the job . . . but *especially* in the church.

## What the Word Says                What the Word Says to Me

*Prophecy*:
Pursue love, and desire spiritual gifts, but especially that

you may prophesy. (1 Cor. 14:1)

*Ministering or Serving:*
For you, brethren, have been called to liberty; only do not use liberty as an opportunity for the flesh, but through love serve one another. (Gal. 5:13)

*Teaching:*
For this reason I have sent Timothy to you, who is my beloved and faithful son in the Lord, who will remind you of my ways in Christ, as I teach everywhere in every church. (1 Cor. 4:17)

*Exhorting:*
Beware, brethren, lest there be in any of you an evil heart of unbelief in departing from the living God; but exhort one another daily, while it is called "Today," lest any of you be hardened through the deceitfulness of sin. (Heb. 3:12–13)

*Giving:*
[Jesus said], "Give and it will be given to you: good measure, pressed down, shaken together, and running over will be put into your bosom." (Luke 6:38)

*Leading:*
One who rules his own house
well, having his children in
submission with all reverence
(for if a man does not know
how to rule his own house,
how will he take care of the
church of God?) (1 Tim. 3:4)

-----------------------------
-----------------------------
-----------------------------
-----------------------------
-----------------------------
-----------------------------
-----------------------------

*Mercy:*
Therefore, as the elect of God,
holy and beloved, put on tender mercies, kindness,
humility, meekness, long-
suffering. (Col. 3:12)

-----------------------------
-----------------------------
-----------------------------
-----------------------------
-----------------------------

- *In your life, have you identified your particular ministry gift?*
  _____

  _____

- *If you have identified your particular gift, how do you feel
  about your particular gift?*
  _____

  _____

- *In what ways are you feeling challenged in your spirit?*
  _____

  _____

## Discovering Your Particular Gift

If you are not readily able to identify your own motivational
gift at this point, do not be alarmed. In the lessons that follow,
you will have ample opportunity to zero in on your specific

gift. Recognize at this point that there are several reasons that Christians don't seem to recognize their own gifts.

1. *They may have a "cloudy" relationship with God.* They may not have accepted Jesus Christ as their Savior. They may not know that as a believer in Jesus Christ, they have been indwelled by the Holy Spirit or that they have been given a ministry gift. They may be unsure about their position in Christ Jesus. If any of these issues are relevant to your life, I encourage you to take action. Accept Jesus Christ as your Savior. Invite the Holy Spirit to dwell within you, and state openly your reliance upon the Holy Spirit to teach you and guide you daily. Study God's Word to discover your position in Christ Jesus. (See the *InTouch* Bible study on "Living in His Sufficiency.")

2. *They may not be involved in service to others.* Much of what we discover about ourselves and particularly about our ministry gift is learned *as* we attempt to help others.

3. *They may be attempting to imitate another person*—perhaps someone they admire or perhaps the person who led them to Christ. As long as we are trying to copy the ministry gift of another person, we will not be in a position fully to recognize, embrace, or develop our own gift from God.

4. *They may have failed to recognize fully the motivation for their own actions.* Many people never ask why about the things they do or say. Discovering one's motivational gift requires a certain degree of introspection and self-examination.

5. *They may be confused about the difference between* ministry *and* gift. Ministry is a specific act of service to others. Working with the children's choir and feeding the homeless are two examples of ministry. A ministry gift is the *motivation* that leads us to engage in a particular facet of ministry. For example, the person who is involved in the children's choir may have the gift of leading—such a person is likely to administer and organize the program, and may very well be the choirmaster. Another person involved in the children's choir may have a gift of service—such a person may be the one who makes sure that the

choir robes are clean and pressed, or that refreshments are available to the children after the rehearsals.

6. *They may have a false understanding that only full-time clergy and staff members in a church are gifted or qualified for ministry.* The ministry gifts are given to *all* members of the church. Every person has been gifted and is commanded by God to use his or her gift. Church roles are identified elsewhere in the Scriptures as apostles, prophets, evangelists, and pastors and teachers. Even within the church roles, a person will have a tendency to gravitate toward and to minister out of a particular motivational gift.

- *In what ways are you feeling challenged about the discovery of your ministry gift?*

  _____

  _____

## The Way the Gifts Work Together

The motivational gifts are designed to work together—to complement each other and to be joined together in productive ways that bring benefit to the whole body of believers. As we each develop and exercise our motivational gifts, we bring refinement and balance to the body as a whole. The framework for the use of our gifts was also given by Paul. Three key words were emphasized by Jesus, Paul, and by other New Testament writers regarding the way we treat one another and minister to one another:

- *Love*—We each are to treat others with love at all times. Love must be our attitude, the tone of our voice, the purpose for our actions, and the goal we seek in all relationships.
- *Humility*—We each are to treat others with respect, gentleness, and patience.
- *Peace*—We are to create an overall atmosphere of peace

and reconciliation within the church. The ministry gifts are never intended to divide God's people, but rather to heal, restore, nurture, unify, and build up God's people into a strong and vibrant whole.

The exercise of gifts *without* love and humility results in our coming across as "sounding brass or a clanging cymbal"—obnoxious sounds that interrupt and bring discord. Love, however, builds up and brings peace.

| What the Word Says | What the Word Says to Me |
|---|---|
| [Jesus said], "This is My commandment, that you love one another as I have loved you." (John 15:12) | |
| Be kindly affectionate to one another with brotherly love, in honor giving preference to one another. (Rom. 12:10) | |
| Through love serve one another. (Gal. 5:13) | |
| I, therefore, the prisoner of the Lord, beseech you to walk worthy of the calling with which you were called, with all lowliness and gentleness, with longsuffering, bearing with one another in love, endeavoring to keep the unity of the Spirit in the bond of peace. (Eph. 4:1–3) | |
| And let the peace of God rule | |

in your hearts, to which also
you were called in one body.
(Col. 3:15)

Earnestly desire the best gifts.
And yet I show you a more
excellent way. Though I speak
with the tongues of men and of
angels, but have not love, I
have become sounding brass or
a clanging cymbal. And though
I have the gift of prophecy, and
understand all mysteries and
all knowledge, and though I
have all faith, so that I could
remove mountains, but have
not love, I am nothing. And
though I bestow all my goods
to feed the poor, and though I
give my body to be burned,
but have not love, it profits me
nothing. (1 Cor. 12:31;
13:1–3)

Any exercise of our motivational gifts without love brings no
benefit to us or others. Truly, for our ministry gifts to be effective and to be a blessing, we must choose to love, we must
work for peace, and we must remain humble in our relationships with others.

When we each use our motivational gifts in God-desired
ways, we experience minimal weariness and maximal effec-
tiveness. It is as we develop and use our ministry gifts that we
find deep inner satisfaction and contentment—the purpose for
our life is fulfilled, and we have a great sense of meaning.

- *What new insights do you have into the motivational gifts?*

  _____

  _____

- *In what ways are you feeling challenged in your spirit?*

  _____

  _____

# LESSON 3

# THE GIFT OF PROPHECY

Do you find that you can't remain quiet or sit still when you know you are hearing a lie or are in the presence of evil? Do you have a clear-cut understanding of what God considers to be right and wrong? You may have been given the gift of prophecy.

Prophets are those who speak the truth. Many people have an understanding of prophecy as "foretelling the future." The greater meaning and more general meaning for this term in the Bible is the "forth-telling" of proclaiming those principles of God which are true now and forever.

The genuine prophet of God *must* speak the truth—he cannot remain quiet in the face of a lie or any form of deceit, or in the face of an error against God's Word or God's nature. The prophet is very often a person who sees things in black-and-white, right-or-wrong terms. He functions particularly in the presence of injustice and out of a motivation to set things right or to get the church back on the right track.

Peter is a man in the Scriptures who functioned in the role of the prophet. As the focus for our study about those who have the gift of prophecy, we'll identify the general nature of the gift of prophecy, and in each case, look at an instance in which Peter manifested this gift.

**1.** *The gift of prophecy goes head-to-head in its confrontation of evil, hypocrisy, error, and false conclusions or judgments.* On the day of Pentecost, when confronted with those who were accusing Jesus' followers of being drunk with new wine, it was Peter who took action.

> But Peter, standing up with the eleven, raised his voice and said to them, "Men of Judea and all who dwell in Jerusalem, let this be known to you, and heed my words. For these are not drunk, as you suppose, since it is only the third hour of the day. But this is what was spoken by the prophet Joel." (Acts 2:14–16)

**2.** *The gift of prophecy often reveals the character and motives of others, especially those motives that are deceitful or hypocritical.* When Ananias and Sapphira conspired to lie about the gift they were making to the early church, Peter was the one who confronted them. We read in Acts 5:1–4 Peter's response to their lie:

> But a certain man named Ananias, with Sapphira his wife, sold a possession. And he kept back part of the proceeds, his wife also being aware of it, and brought a certain part and laid it at the apostles' feet. But Peter said, "Ananias, why has Satan filled your heart to lie to the Holy Spirit and keep back part of the price of the land for yourself? While it remained, was it not your own? And after it was sold, was it not in your own control? Why have you conceived this thing in your heart? You have not lied to men but to God."

- *Have you ever had a confrontational experience with a prophet, or witnessed a prophet in a confrontational situation? Was the prophecy given in a spirit of love, humility, and peace? How did you feel? What were the results?*

_____

_____

**3.** *The gift of prophecy requires the prophet to be honest about himself and to seek correction for his own error.* The genuine prophet of God is a person who will always want the truth to reign in his own life, just as he demands truth from others and in the lives of others. It is a false prophet who requires truth in others but is unwilling to face or confront the truth of his own life. When Jesus commanded Peter to launch into the deep and let down his nets for a catch, which Peter did reluctantly and with doubt, the result was a net-breaking load of fish. Peter recognized his own doubt and failure in this situation and responded as a genuine prophet responds. "He fell down at Jesus' knees, saying, 'Depart from me, for I am a sinful man, O Lord'" (Luke 5:8).

**4.** *The gift of prophecy is often voiced as a defense of the church, God's people, God's programs, or God's nature.* The genuine prophet is a strong advocate of God's work, although he never takes credit for what God does—to do so would make him party to a lie. The genuine prophet stands up for the veracity of God's Word and the manifestations of God's Spirit. The genuine prophet always points to Jesus as Savior, Deliverer, Healer, and Lord.

After Peter and John had spoken to a lame man at the Beautiful Gate of the Temple, and the man had been healed by God, many began to respond to Peter and John more than to the Lord. Peter was quick to set the matter in proper order. When Peter saw it, he responded to the people:

> Men of Israel, why do you marvel at this? Or why look so intently at us, as though by our own power or godliness we had made this man walk? The God of Abraham, Isaac, and Jacob, the God of our fathers, glorified His Servant Jesus . . . and His name, through faith in His name, has made this man strong, whom you see and know. Yes, the faith which comes through Him has given him this perfect soundness in the presence of you all. (Acts 3:12–13, 16)

5. *The gift of prophecy functions without regard to personal consequences for the prophet.* The genuine prophet sees the consequences of evil that go unchecked and is much more concerned that those consequences be averted than he is concerned about his own welfare.

When Peter was imprisoned for proclaiming Jesus as the Messiah, those who had imprisoned him commanded Peter and John not to speak at all nor to teach in the name of Jesus, and they also threatened them with severe punishment. Here is how Peter responded:

> But Peter and John answered and said to them, "Whether it is right in the sight of God to listen to you more than to God, you judge. For we cannot but speak the things which we have seen and heard." (Acts 4:19–20)

• *How have you* felt *as you have read Peter's words?*

_____

_____

• *After reading these five passages of Scripture, what new insights do you have into the role and nature of the gift of prophecy?*

_____

_____

## The Characteristics of a Prophet

As you may have concluded from reading about Peter, a true prophet in action, these are among the characteristics of a person who has the motivational gift of prophecy:

• *Boldness.* Prophets are often very bold and direct. They may come across as being fearless or blunt, when in fact they are actually fearful only that God will be displeased with them for any hesitancy in confronting a lie.

- *Simple answers that may seem simplistic.* Prophets not only see problems in black-and-white terms, but they tend to "cut to the chase" in the solutions they offer. They are quick to want "bottom-line" facts and to take immediate action.
- *Persuasiveness.* Prophets usually seek to do their utmost to evoke change They will use whatever means are available to them to argue for the truth.
- *A desire for immediate change.* Prophets have little tolerance for lengthy discussion, group consensus, phased-in changes, or slow processes.
- *Strong dependence on the Scriptures.* The genuine prophet bases his understanding of truth on the Scriptures.
- *Loyalty.* Prophets have a deep and abiding commitment to the truth and to the Lord. This devotion is "to the death." Prophets may seem fearless in their commitment.
- *Brokenness.* The genuine prophet has a willingness to be broken by God so that they can be more closely conformed to the likeness of Christ Jesus.
- *Quick judgment and speech.* Prophets often come across as reactionary and impulsive. Because they see right and wrong clearly and have no tolerance for lies, they are quick to confront lies and errors.

As you read through the passages identified below, note the evidence for each of these characteristics of a prophet's nature.

| What the Word Says | What the Word Says to Me |
|---|---|
| Acts 2:17–40 (Peter's address on the Day of Pentecost) | ----------------------------- <br> ----------------------------- |
| Acts 3:12–26 (Peter's address to the masses in the Temple) | ----------------------------- <br> ----------------------------- |

Acts 4:8–12 (Peter's address to
the rulers, elders, and scribes)

_____

_____

Acts 10:34–48 (Peter's address
at Cornelius's house)

_____

_____

- *In your experience, can you identify a person or persons whom you know to have the ministry gift of prophecy? Do you yourself have this gift?*

- *What tends to be your emotional reaction to those who have this ministry gift? Why is it especially important that this gift operate in a spirit of love, humility, and peace?*

## Vital but Few in the Church

Prophets are vital for the church, but because they are so confrontational and so direct in what they say, prophets are also few in number in the church. Prophets are like a strong spice—they give flavor and identity, as well as direction and guidance, but a little goes a long way.

We also must recognize that Satan targets prophets in a special way because they can be so effective for the gospel when they are operating under the guidance of the Holy Spirit and in a spirit of humility, love, and peace. They can also be devastating and bring reproach upon the church when they function "in the flesh" and are not one-hundred-percent reliant upon the Holy Spirit at all times.

We must pray for those who are prophets to be strong and true to God's Word. Above all, we must test their words against the Word of God and heed what they say when they accurately reveal error or deceit in our midst.

## Jesus—Our Role Model

Finally, we must recognize that Jesus was a prophet. He is the supreme role model for all prophets to follow. He spoke the truth of God always, regardless of circumstances or consequences, but He always spoke God's truth with love as His motivation and always knew the cleansing of human hearts and reconciliation with God the Father as His goal.

### What the Word Says

Read Jesus' words to chief priest and elders of the people in Matthew 21:31–44, and their response below:

When the chief priests and Pharisees heard His parables, they perceived that He was speaking of them. But when they sought to lay hands on Him, they feared the multitudes, because they took Him for a prophet. (Matt. 21:45–46)

He who prophesies speaks edification and exhortation and comfort to men . . . let all things be done for edification. (1 Cor. 14:3, 26)

Brethren, desire earnestly to prophesy . . . let all things be done decently and in order. (1 Cor. 14:39–40)

### What the Word Says to Me

----------------------------
----------------------------
----------------------------
----------------------------

----------------------------
----------------------------
----------------------------
----------------------------
----------------------------
----------------------------
----------------------------
----------------------------

----------------------------
----------------------------
----------------------------
----------------------------
----------------------------

----------------------------
----------------------------
----------------------------
----------------------------

• *What new insights do you have into the ministry gift of prophecy?*

_____

_____

• *In what ways are you feeling challenged in your spirit?*

_____

_____

# LESSON 4

# THE GIFT OF SERVICE

Are you motivated to pursue practical areas of service to others? Are you concerned with the practical, tangible work associated with a project? Do you enjoy doing things with your hands and in association with other people? You may be a person who has been given the motivational gift of service.

In the Scriptures, Timothy—the spiritual son and coworker of the apostle Paul—is a man who had the gift of serving. He is an excellent role model for us.

## Characteristics of the Gift of Serving

The gift of service has a number of facets to it, among which are the following five characteristics:

1. *A person with the gift of service is alert to practical needs and has a desire to meet them.* The person with this gift has a heightened sensitivity to those in need and has a compassionate heart that almost can't *help* but reach out in an attempt to meet the need he perceives. Their greatest satisfaction comes in seeing a need met, in part or in full, through their efforts.

The person with a gift of service has a great desire to bring pleasure and joy to others. One manifestation of this desire is usually a great memory concerning the likes and dislikes of other people.

Persons with this gift often go far beyond what is required

to meet a need. They truly seek to *bless* others, not simply to provide the bare minimum.

Paul wrote this about Timothy: "I trust in the Lord Jesus to send Timothy to you shortly, that I also may be encouraged when I know your state. For I have no one like-minded, who will sincerely care for your state" (Phil. 2:19–20).

Paul didn't know anybody who would care for the Philippians with the same tenderness, love, and diligence as Timothy.

Paul also was on the receiving end of Timothy's ministry of service. Notice what he says to Timothy in 2 Timothy 4:9–13:

> Be diligent to come to me quickly . . . Get Mark and bring him with you, for he is useful to me for ministry . . . Bring the cloak that I left with Carpus at Troas when you come—and the books, especially the parchments.

Paul knew that he could trust Timothy with these very practical concerns because Timothy was gifted to serve in this way. We also find in Acts 19:20 that Timothy was one of two people who are identified as those who "ministered" to Paul. Timothy was a man who cared for Paul's practical needs and who assisted him in every way possible.

- *In your life, have you met a person who truly has the gift of serving? Do you yourself have this ministry gift?*

_____

_____


2. *The person with a gift of serving has joy when he knows the service frees another person to engage more fully in the ministry to which he has been called.* Those with a gift of service delight in preparing the background details and doing the backstage work that allows others to perform to the best of their ability. Because they take joy in the accomplishments and success of others, they often are dismayed or disturbed when they see the

person they are serving squandering time or devoting energy to things that are unproductive or outside their ministry gifts. On the other hand, if they see the person whom they are serving focusing energy and doing the work to which God has called him or her, they have great delight and a deep feeling of satisfaction.

The person with this gift is very generous in giving time, energy, abilities, and effort, and especially so if worthwhile projects are undertaken and completed as a result.

At times, others may mistake the motives of the person with a gift of service because the person is always eager to undertake another project or to tackle another need.

- *How do you feel when you are a part of a team of people who is doing work unto the Lord with diligence and faithfulness?*

---

---

**3.** *The person with a gift of service often tends to ignore his own needs and to overextend personal energy and strength.* Those with this gift are often so concerned with getting a job done that they overlook the passing of time, or the meeting of their personal needs, including health. A mother with this gift of service will often work untiringly long into the night to meet the needs of her family, even to the neglect of her own physical needs.

Paul wrote to Timothy, "No longer drink only water, but use a little wine for your stomach's sake and your frequent infirmities" (1 Tim. 5:23). Paul sent Timothy to some very difficult places to minister. For example, he sent him to Crete—one of the most difficult places to preach the gospel and nurture a group of new believers. In writing to Titus, Paul quoted a Cretan who said about his own people, "Cretans are always liars, evil beasts, lazy gluttons." Paul added, "This testimony is true" (Titus 1:12–13). Timothy no doubt encountered numerous stressful and difficult situations and people in the course of his ministry on the island of Crete, and yet he was so faithful in his ministry and in his serving the people that he neglected his own health.

The downside for the person with the gift of service is that he may be so highly motivated to help another person that he overlooks the emotional needs of those in his own family. He may get so wrapped up in meeting the needs of those he sees as genuinely "needy" that he neglects the less obvious and more basic needs of those closest to him.

- *In your life, have you met a person who serves others to the neglect of his or her own needs? What was the result?*

 

 

**4.** *The person with a gift of serving has a need to be appreciated for his or her service to confirm that it is necessary, valued, and beneficial.* Persons with this gift have no desire to waste their time or efforts on things that will be of little use or benefit. They are so concerned with the overall success of a project, organization, or ministry that they do not want to waste any of their own energies on things that will be of little consequence.

The person with this gift is motivated by praise and appreciation. They will want to do even more for the person who acknowledges and is thankful for their contribution.

Paul was quick to praise Timothy and to acknowledge his efforts. He wrote to the Corinthians:

> And if Timothy comes, see that he may be with you without fear; for he does the work of the Lord, as I also do. Therefore let no one despise him. (1 Cor. 16:10–11)

Always ask yourself as you work with others who may have this gift of service, "How can I show my appreciation to this person who is giving so much of his time, talent, and energy?"

• *In what ways are you feeling challenged in your spirit?*

_____

_____

5. *The person with a gift of serving has a strong desire to be with other people.* Those with this gift are not loners—they are "people persons." They enjoy being with people because the more people they meet, the more opportunities they have to discover and respond to needs in the lives of others.

In Acts 19 and 20, we find Timothy mentioned several times. Each time he is mentioned with someone else. In Acts 19:22 he is mentioned with Erastus, and in Acts 20:4 Timothy is part of a team that is working with Paul, including Sopater, Aristarchus, Secundus, Gaius, Tychicus, and Trophimus. People with the gift of service find their greatest sense of fulfillment in being with people and relating to them in practical and helpful ways.

The person with a gift of service doesn't need his or her name in headlines. He doesn't need to be in the spotlight. But he does need to be in relationships with other people.

6. *Those with the gift of service feel that they* must *respond to the practical needs they see.* They quickly perceive needs and once they have perceived a need, they are compelled to act. They *must* act. They cannot sit still in the face of a need.

At times, the person with a gift of service may seem pushy because he is so willing to volunteer and to get started with a task. They almost have the attitude, "If you just get out of my way and cut all the red tape, I'll get this done for you in no time." They have little tolerance for rules and procedures seen as unnecessary for the completion of a task.

7. *Those with the gift of service are most effective in working on short-range projects.* They gravitate naturally toward projects that can be completed in relatively short periods of time. People with the gift of serving tend to be frustrated by long-range projects; they need immediate signs of progress to validate the

effort and time they are giving. If a project is going to take five years, it should be turned over to a person who has a gift of leadership or administration; then that person should recruit those with the gift of service who can take smaller pieces of that project and see them to completion.

8. *Those with this gift of service often feel very unqualified and inadequate for ministry.* They often do not perceive that they are "ministers"—they simply see themselves as practical, can-do people.

Paul encouraged Timothy in this way on one occasion: "This charge I commit to you, son Timothy, according to the prophecies previously made concerning you, that by them you may wage the good warfare, having faith and a good conscience" (1 Tim. 1:18–19).

Timothy may very well have been discouraged into thinking that he was unqualified for the task Paul had given him. Paul reminds him of prophecies that confirm Timothy is doing what God desires him to do, and that he has what it takes to engage in successful spiritual warfare.

- *What new insights do you have into the characteristics of those who have the gift of service?*

---

---

## Five Things to Guard Against

The person with the gift of serving has to be especially sensitive to these potentially negative aspects of service:

1. *The person with the gift of serving must guard against becoming discouraged if others fail to appreciate his service.* Always, service is *as unto the Lord.* People will disappoint us in their lack of appreciation and fail to acknowledge acts of service; God sees all of our acts of service and He is a faithful rewarder of those who serve with diligence and faithfulness.

2. *The person with the gift of serving must guard against doing so*

*much for others that he never gives others an opportunity to give in return.* My own mother had a great gift of service. She was so good at anticipating needs in others that very often she was halfway finished with meeting a need before I or another person had an opportunity to voice the need! Learn to receive from others. If you fail to do so, you will be robbing others of the rewards that come from giving.

**3.** *The person with the gift of serving must be very sensitive to what God is attempting to teach or to reveal to another person.* At times, we can be too quick to meet needs in the lives of others—to the point where we negate the lesson that God is attempting to convey to them.

**4.** *The person with the gift of serving must remain attentive to personal spiritual growth and to the disciplines of prayer, praise, and reading of Scripture.* He must fight the tendency to be so busy with practical considerations that spiritual growth suffers. Martha, a friend of Jesus and sister to Lazarus and Mary, was a woman who was very concerned about serving. Jesus recognized the value of her gift and her service, but encouraged her in saying, "Martha, Martha, you are worried and troubled about many things. But one thing is needed, and Mary has chosen that good part, which will not be taken away from her" (Luke 10:41–42). Jesus called Martha to a time of relaxing in His presence, listening to Him, and enjoying His fellowship.

**5.** *The person with this gift must avoid the tendency to get sidetracked by what appear to be more "urgent" needs—to the point where the original need may not be met.*

- *In what ways are you feeling challenged in your spirit? Are there ways you might help another person who has the gift of serving to guard against these potentially negative consequences in the employment of their gift?*

---

---

## Hallmarks of Godly Service

The Bible admonishes us in a number of ways about how to engage in godly service one to another. We are to serve in this way:

- *Be alert.* Ask the Holy Spirit to show you precisely what needs you are to meet and how best to meet them.
- *Be hospitable.* Show kindness and consideration to others as you serve them. Be gracious to others in the way you speak to them and assist them.
- *Be generous.* Give generously, but be aware that you are not responsible for meeting all the needs of another person—indeed, you are incapable of being the sole source of supply, answers, or provision for another person. Only God can meet *all* the needs in a person's life.
- *Be joyful.* Do your service with a joyful heart. Inspire others to praise and give thanks to God.
- *Be flexible.* Should the Lord reveal to you a different way of serving or an unusual avenue for service that you have not pursued before, be willing to obey the Lord explicitly.
- *Be available.* Do not hide behind false humility if you are asked to minister in a way that seems a challenge to you. Virtually every type of ministry *needs* those who are willing and gifted to *serve.*
- *Be diligent in seeing a project to its completion.* Don't allow yourself to become sidetracked or to spread yourself too thin.

| What the Word Says | What the Word Says to Me |
| --- | --- |
| With goodwill doing service, as to the Lord, and not to men, knowing that whatever good anyone does, he will receive the same from the Lord. (Eph. 6:7–8) | _____ _____ _____ _____ _____ _____ |

Not lagging in diligence, fervent in spirit, serving the Lord. (Rom. 12:11)

Serving the Lord with all humility. (Acts 20:19)

Set in order the things that are lacking. (Titus 1:5)

Be hospitable to one another without grumbling. (1 Peter 4:9)

Therefore, to him who knows to do good and does not do it, to him it is sin. (James 4:17)

Now may our Lord Jesus Christ Himself, and our God and Father . . . comfort your hearts and establish you in every good word and work. (2 Thess. 2:16–17)

And whatever you do, do it heartily, as to the Lord and not to men, knowing that from the Lord you will receive the reward of the inheritance; for you serve the Lord Christ. (Col. 3:23–24)

Do all things without complaining and disputing, that you may become blameless and harmless. (Phil. 2:14–15)

## Jesus—The Greatest Servant of All

One of the names given to Jesus was that of Servant. He taught His disciples:

> I have given you an example, that you should do as I have done to you. Most assuredly, I say to you, a servant is not greater than his master; nor is he who is sent greater than he who sent him. If you know these things, blessed are you if you do them. (John 13:15–17)

Jesus said this to His disciples after He had washed their feet—a lowly task usually done by household servants. As Jesus humbled Himself to serve, so we must humble ourselves to serve. No act of service to another human being in need should ever be considered too lowly or "beneath our dignity."

| What the Word Says | What the Word Says to Me |
| --- | --- |
| Let this mind be in you which was also in Christ Jesus, who, being in the form of God, did not consider it robbery to be equal with God, but made Himself of no reputation, taking the form of a bondservant, and coming in the likeness of men. And being found in appearance as a man, He humbled Himself and became obedient to the point of death, even the death of the cross. Therefore God also has highly exalted Him and given Him the name which is above every name. (Phil. 2:5–9) | |

As Christ also loved the
church, and gave Himself for
her. (Eph. 5:25)

-------------------------------
-------------------------------
-------------------------------

In employing our gift of service, we must always keep Jesus as our role model. We are to serve *in His name, for His glory,* and *in the same manner of love* He showed to others. Jesus served with a sacrificial heart. He gave His all. He calls those who are given the gift of service to do the same.

- *What new insights do you have into the gift of serving?*

  _____

  _____

- *In what ways are you feeling challenged in your spirit?*

  _____

  _____

# LESSON 5

# THE GIFT OF TEACHING

Are you concerned with accuracy when the Word of God is taught or interpreted? Are you concerned that the truth be passed on to the next generation or to those who currently are lacking in understanding and wisdom? Do you desire to see the lives of others changed as the result of information being given to them? You may be a person who has been given the motivational gift of teaching.

Those with other gifts may *be* teachers, but their motivation for teaching is not the pursuit of God's truth. A person may become a Sunday school teacher in the preschool department out of love and compassion for the children. That person is motivated to teach by a gift of mercy. Another person may be motivated to teach because he is concerned that too much emphasis is being placed upon discussion of the application of Scripture and not enough on the black-and-white, right-and-wrong absolutes of the Bible. That person is motivated to teach out of a ministry gift of prophecy. The person who is gifted to teach desires to teach and is motivated solely because he or she loves the truth and wants to impart the truth of God's Word with accuracy and fullness of understanding to others.

One of the foremost teachers in the Bible is Luke. Just look at how he begins his Gospel account:

Inasmuch as many have taken in hand to set in order a narrative of those things which have been fulfilled among us, just as those who from the beginning were eyewitnesses and ministers of the word delivered them to us, it seemed good to me also, having had perfect understanding of all things from the very first, to write to you an orderly account, most excellent Theophilus, that you may know the certainty of those things in which you were instructed. (Luke 1:1–4)

Doesn't Luke *sound* like a teacher? He says of himself that he is an expert, that his understanding is "perfect," and that his account will be orderly. His desire is that Theophilus "know with certainty"—in other words, to know with exactness of detail. Luke's Gospel as well as the book of Acts are highly detailed accounts. They are intended to *teach* the truth with certainty that Jesus was the Christ.

- *Do you know someone who is gifted to be a teacher? Have you received the motivational gift of teaching?*

  _____

  _____

## Characteristics of the Gift of Teaching

Teaching was considered a highly valued profession in both Jewish and Greek circles. To be a teacher within the early church was also an exalted position—few were called teachers. A great responsibility was placed upon teachers to be accurate, wise, diligent in their research, and skilled in their ability to present information. Then as now, the gift of teaching was expected to display the following seven characteristics:

1. *The gift of teaching includes a great concern with a systematic sequence.* Teachers seek to present material in a way that is easy for others to follow. Luke notes that he is going to write an "orderly account." Another translation of those

words would be "consecutive order." The teacher lays out his material so it all points toward specific themes, which taken together convey the main point.

2. *The gift of teaching includes a concern with the accuracy of words and the use of language.* A teacher is concerned with precise definitions and shades of meaning. A teacher can be irritating at times because he or she is always asking, "What do you mean by that? What does that mean to you?" He wants to hear and speak with accuracy.

3. *The gift of teaching includes a delight in researching and reporting as many details as possible.* The Gospel of Luke contains more details about key events than any other Gospel. Luke sees meaning in details. The person gifted in teaching delights in his own study of a passage of Scripture or in his own research. He takes great joy in seeing meaning in factual details that may have been overlooked by others. Once this information has been acquired, the teacher longs to share everything he knows. At times that can be more information than others want or need to hear, but the teacher feels compelled to "teach all."

No other Gospel writer tells us about the birth of Jesus as Luke tells us. Nearly three chapters of His Gospel are devoted to the birth of Jesus—he not only tells the story of Mary and Joseph, but also the stories of Zacharias and Elizabeth, and Simeon and Anna. He does not deal only with the facts of the story, but with dialogue, monologue, and references to the Old Testament.

4. *The gift of teaching includes a great interest in knowing as much as possible about a subject being studied.* A teacher never tires of delving into a chosen area of study, or engaging in multiple studies with increasing depth over time. The teacher desires that all of the information he presents is accurate, valid, and verifiable. Traditional historical accounts tell us that Luke took several years to research his Gospel, talking to numerous people who had known Jesus personally.

5. *The gift of teaching is concerned with the acquisition of knowledge and understanding, both of which are vital to wisdom.* The prophet is concerned that a person make the right decision and recognize fully what is at stake if the wrong decision is made. A changed life is the goal. The person who exhorts is concerned that a person understand the step-by-step process necessary to reach a particular goal, and admonishes others that no step and no necessary requisite behavior be omitted or overlooked. A correction is the goal. The teacher, by comparison, is concerned that a person *know* the Bible and the commandments of God with precision and full understanding. Acquisition of knowledge is the goal, as Luke wrote to Theophilus, "that you may know the certainty of those things in which you were instructed" (Luke 1:4).

6. *The gift of teaching is primarily concerned with fact, not illustration or application.* Teachers are rarely impulsive and often reject emotional material or illustrations. They nearly always have a tendency toward logic and organization. They are not likely to delight in lengthy discussion. In fact, they can quickly become irritated with those who talk too much, and especially so if the person doesn't seem to know what he or she is talking about!

7. *The gift of teaching is usually pursued in a very systematic way.* Most teachers have developed a personal "method" for doing research and presenting information to others. They develop a means for determining what is true. They sift all things necessary for their method before drawing a conclusion.

• *How do you feel when you hear someone who truly is gifted to be a teacher present the Word of God?*

_____

_____

• *What new insights do you have into the gift of teaching?*

_____

_____

## Words of Caution for the Teacher

The goal of a teacher within the Body of Christ must be the presentation of Jesus Christ, with the intent that others "grow up" in their faith to be more and more like Jesus. The purpose is not simply to convince others of the teacher's own intellect or degree of information, but rather to convince others to accept Christ Jesus and become more mature in their Christian lives.

*A teacher must seek to be a good communicator.* Too often teachers are content to present the facts as they have studied them, without making their subject matter of interest or application to their students. For true "learning" to occur, one must not only be a good researcher and organizer of information, but an effective communicator—a person who knows how to convey information in a way that will captivate the will and desire of those who hear him speak or read his writing.

*A teacher must be open to new means of presenting information.* Teachers often have a tendency to be too narrow in their interpretation of what is "information," "fact," or "knowledge." They see straightforward declarative statements as more desirable than the telling of stories, even though stories are an excellent vehicle for conveying the truth of God's Word. Jesus, of course, was a master at parable-telling, the use of stories to convey spiritual truth. Most teachers can benefit from incorporating more illustrations and applications into their factual presentations.

*A teacher must not get hung up on small errors in detail.* Too often teachers dismiss an entire presentation solely on the basis of one particular error. They need to be able to sift error from truth.

*A teacher must always be open to the intuitive spiritual leading of the Holy Spirit to discern truth.* Truth is more than facts. Many teachers rely mostly on their own intellectual abilities and skills to evaluate situations. They must also be open to hearing what the Holy Spirit may whisper into their hearts and minds.

*A teacher must always look for the big picture.* Some teachers become too narrow in their approach and fail to see the broad background or the general direction. We each must be open at all times to have an enlarged vision of what it is that the Lord is desiring to do in our world today and how He may desire for us to play a role.

*A teacher must never substitute "academic degrees" for genuine wisdom from God.* I have met numerous people who have had very little formal education but who have had a great understanding of both God's Word and the ways in which God works in the human heart. I have also met people who have had a string of degrees behind their names who could barely communicate with sense and who had no understanding of God. Formal education is not a "qualifier" for the gift of teaching. On the basis of formal education, we must never look down on those who have this genuine motivational gift—and neither must we exalt those who call themselves teachers solely because they have completed degrees but have no gift of God for teaching.

## What the Word Says

Him we preach, warning every man and teaching every man in all wisdom, that we may present every man perfect in Christ Jesus. (Col. 1:28)

These things we also speak, not in words which man's wisdom teaches but which the Holy Spirit teaches, comparing

## What the Word Says to Me

_____

_____

_____

_____

_____

_____

_____

_____

_____

spiritual things with spiritual.
(1 Cor. 2:13)

-----------------------------
-----------------------------

Let the word of Christ dwell
in you richly in all wisdom,
teaching and admonishing one
another in psalms and hymns
and spiritual songs, singing
with grace in your hearts to
the Lord. And whatever you
do in word or deed, do all in
the name of the Lord Jesus,
giving thanks to God the
Father through Him. (Col.
3:16–17)

-----------------------------
-----------------------------
-----------------------------
-----------------------------
-----------------------------
-----------------------------
-----------------------------
-----------------------------
-----------------------------
-----------------------------
-----------------------------

- *What new insights do you have into the gift of teaching?*

-------------------------------------------------

-------------------------------------------------

## Qualities of the Godly Teacher

Those who have been gifted as teachers are challenged by the Scriptures to exhibit these behaviors:

- *Self-control*—an ability to focus on the issue at hand and to avoid all detours as they prepare the lesson they are to teach
- *Reverence and respect for the Word of God*—seeking the truth of God's Word, never approaching God's Word with the intent of disputing it or denying its validity
- *Diligence and thoroughness*—sticking to the study and research until they have a thorough knowledge of the subject and have prepared diligently the best lesson possible
- *Dependability*—so that others can always rely upon them to "rightly divide" the Word of truth

Those who operate under the guidance of the Holy Spirit and who recognize that they are gifted as teachers will not find teaching to be a burden—rather, these behaviors will be the natural way they respond to any opportunity to teach.

Psalm 119 may very well be the psalm of the gifted teacher. Note below the references from this psalm that relate to a love and respect for God's Word. To the person gifted in teaching, there is no greater joy than to study the Bible and then share what has been learned.

| What the Word Says | What the Word Says to Me |
|---|---|
| Remind them of these things, charging them before the Lord not to strive about words to no profit, to the ruin of the hearers. Be diligent to present yourself approved to God, a worker who does not need to be ashamed, rightly dividing the word of truth. But shun profane and idle babblings, for they will increase to more ungodliness. (2 Tim. 2:14–16) | ------------------------------- ------------------------------- ------------------------------- ------------------------------- ------------------------------- ------------------------------- ------------------------------- ------------------------------- ------------------------------- ------------------------------- ------------------------------- |
| I will delight myself in Your statutes; I will not forget Your Word. (Ps. 119:16) | ------------------------------- ------------------------------- ------------------------------- ------------------------------- |
| Your servant meditates on Your statutes, Your testimonies also are my delight And my counselors. (Ps. 119:23–24) | ------------------------------- ------------------------------- ------------------------------- ------------------------------- ------------------------------- |

Your statutes have been my
songs
In the house of my pilgrimage.
(Ps. 119:54)

------------------------------
------------------------------
------------------------------
------------------------------

The law of Your mouth is better to me
Than thousands of coins of
gold and silver. (Ps. 119:72)

------------------------------
------------------------------
------------------------------
------------------------------

Let my heart be blameless
regarding Your statutes,
That I may not be ashamed.
(Ps. 119:80)

------------------------------
------------------------------
------------------------------
------------------------------

Your word is a lamp to my feet
And a light to my path.
(Ps. 119:105)

------------------------------
------------------------------
------------------------------

My lips shall utter praise,
For You teach me Your statutes.
(Ps. 119:171)

------------------------------
------------------------------
------------------------------

## Being Aware of False Teachers

Jesus made a very clear statement about teaching in
Matthew 5:19:

> Whoever therefore breaks one of the least of these com-
> mandments, and teaches men so, shall be called least
> in the kingdom of heaven; but whoever does and
> teaches them, he shall be called great in the kingdom
> of heaven.

A teacher's first obligation is always to make sure that he personally lives by the truth. It is a false teacher who believes one
thing and says another; a person is also a false teacher if he says
one thing and then lives another. Teachers must recognize that

they always teach not only with their words, but by the example of their lives.

Repeatedly in the Scriptures we find admonitions to be aware of, and therefore to "beware of," false teachers who come into the church. As you read through the verses below, note especially the *behaviors* of those who are false teachers.

| What the Word Says | What the Word Says to Me |
|---|---|
| For there are many insubordinate, both idle talkers and deceivers, especially those of the circumcision, whose mouths must be stopped, who subvert whole households, teaching things which they ought not, for the sake of dishonest gain . . . Rebuke them sharply, that they may be sound in the faith, not giving heed to Jewish fables and commandments of men who turn from the truth. (Titus 1:10–11, 13–14) | ------------------------------<br>------------------------------<br>------------------------------<br>------------------------------<br>------------------------------<br>------------------------------<br>------------------------------<br>------------------------------<br>------------------------------<br>------------------------------<br>------------------------------<br>------------------------------<br>------------------------------<br>------------------------------ |
| Now the purpose of the commandment is love from a pure heart, from a good conscience, and from sincere faith, from which some, having strayed, have turned aside to idle talk, desiring to be teachers of the law, understanding neither what they say nor the things which they affirm. (1 Tim. 1:5–7) | ------------------------------<br>------------------------------<br>------------------------------<br>------------------------------<br>------------------------------<br>------------------------------<br>------------------------------<br>------------------------------<br>------------------------------<br>------------------------------ |

Their message will spread like cancer. Hymenaeus and Phile-tus are of this sort, who have strayed concerning the truth, saying that the resurrection is already past; and they over-throw the faith of some. Nevertheless the solid founda-tion of God stands. (2 Tim. 2:17–19)

For the time will come when they will not endure sound doctrine, but according to their own desires, because they have itching ears, they will heap up for themselves teachers; and they will turn their ears away from the truth, and be turned aside to fables. (2 Tim. 4:3–4)

But there were also false prophets among the people, even as there will be false teachers among you, who will secretly bring in destructive heresies, even denying the Lord who bought them, and bring on themselves swift destruction. And many will fol-low their destructive ways, because of whom the way of truth will be blasphemed. By covetousness they will exploit you with deceptive words. (2 Peter 2:1–3)

• *In what ways are you feeling challenged in your spirit?*

_____

_____

## Jesus was the Master Teacher

The disciples of Jesus frequently addressed Him as "Teacher." Jesus taught by example, by illustration, and by direct presentation of information. He was a consummate teacher in every way. Many of Jesus' miracles followed *teaching* ministry. In the Gospel of Matthew, Jesus' ministry is characterized as one of teaching, preaching, and healing—in each instance, teaching is the first aspect of His ministry that is mentioned. (See Matt. 4:23 as an example.)

Take another look at the passage of Scripture we call "The Sermon on the Mount" (Matt. 5–7). Note the way this "sermon" is prefaced: "And seeing the multitudes, He went up on a mountain, and when He was seated His disciples came to Him. Then He opened His mouth and *taught* them" (Matt. 5:1–2, italics added for emphasis).

I encourage you to read through the Sermon on the Mount and note the many ways in which Jesus embodied and demonstrated "good teaching" to us.

| What the Word Says | What the Word Says to Me |
|---|---|
| And Jesus went about all Galilee, teaching in their synagogues, preaching the gospel of the kingdom, and healing all kinds of sickness and all kinds of disease among the people. (Matt. 4:23) | _____ |
| [Nicodemus] came to Jesus by night and said to Him, "Rabbi, | _____ |

we know that You are a teacher come from God; for no one can do these signs that You do unless God is with him." (John 3:2)

----------------------------------
----------------------------------
----------------------------------
----------------------------------
----------------------------------

Jesus made teaching a part of His great commission to His disciples, saying, "Go therefore and make disciples of all nations . . . teaching them to observe all things that I have commanded you" (Matt. 28:19–20).

What a tremendous responsibility and privilege the "teacher" has within the Body of Christ!

- *What new insights do you have into the motivational ministry gift of teaching?*

  _____

  _____

- *In what ways are you feeling challenged in your spirit?*

  _____

  _____

# LESSON 6

# THE GIFT OF EXHORTATION

Are you vitally concerned about correcting error wherever and whenever you find it? Do you care deeply that those who are about to make mistakes avoid them, and that those who have made mistakes repent of their ways and return to a walk of righteousness before God? You may be a person who has been given the motivational gift of exhortation.

One of the key biblical figures who exemplifies the gift of exhortation is the apostle Paul. Here is the heart of Paul's motivation for ministry:

> Him we preach, warning every man and teaching every man in all wisdom, that we may present every man perfect in Christ Jesus. To this end I also labor, striving according to His working which works in me mightily. (Col. 1:28–29)

The word *warning* in this passage has also been translated as "admonishing" or "exhorting". Exhortation always has an element of caution and concern about it—the exhorter desires to see every believer stay on the straight-and-narrow path that leads to both heavenly and earthly rewards.

• *How do you feel about the word* exhortation?

_____

_____

Before you become alarmed to think that you might be called to all of the perils and suffering that Paul endured or that you might have the responsibility for trailblazing and establishing new ministries as Paul did, let me assure you of two things. First, many are called to exhortation but not all are called to be apostles. Those who have a gift of exhortation may have a quiet and even retiring spirit—but on occasion, they speak with a certainty and finality in their tone that lets everyone around them know that they mean business and that what they say is true and should be heeded. Second, many are called to exhortation in the church but not all are called to exhort large groups of people or even small groups of people. Exhortation often is given in a one-on-one setting. Central to the gift of the exhortation is a heart that desires to encourage other Christians and to see them become all that they can be in Christ Jesus.

Jesus said to His disciples about the work of the Holy Spirit, "I tell you the truth. It is to your advantage that I go away, for if I do not go away, the Helper will not come to you" (John 16:7). The word for "Helper" in this verse is the Greek word *Parakletos*. The Greek word for "exhorter" is also a *parakletos*. The person with a gift of exhortation is called alongside another believer or group of believers to *help* that person or group understand, adhere to, and return to the truth. The person who is a genuine helper is a person who *encourages* others by presence, word, and deed to continue forward in following Jesus Christ.

• *Do you know someone who has been given the gift of exhortation? Have you been given this motivational gift?*

_____

_____

## Jesus—A Portrait of Exhortation

As with all the motivational gifts, Jesus is our role model in the gift of exhortation.

Think about the way Jesus dealt with people in need. He was not a negative person. He never shamed people or belittled them. The only people He did not encourage were the Pharisees and Sadducees because they put great burdens of guilt and shame on others.

Recall specifically how Jesus dealt with a woman who was caught in the act of adultery and who was brought to Him by men who desired to stone her in keeping with the law of Moses. Jesus said to the men who accused her, "He who is without sin among you, let him throw a stone at her first" (John 8:7). When all of her accusers went away, "being convicted by their conscience" (v. 9), Jesus then was left alone with the woman. He said to her, "Woman, where are those accusers of yours? Has no one condemned you?" She said, "No one, Lord." He then said to her, "Neither do I condemn you; go and sin no more" (see John 8:10–11).

*Neither do I condemn you. Go and sin no more.* That is the spirit and those are the hallmark words of the person who exhorts.

Forgiveness. Admonition not to sin. Compassion. An awareness of a person's potential in Christ Jesus. Each of these is to be manifested in exhortation and should be at the core of what an exhorter says and does.

The exhorter should be quick to say, "I accept you. I love in you in Christ Jesus. I believe in who God created you to be and who He is calling and preparing you to be as His beloved child. I recognize that you have sinned, but I forgive you. Now, go and sin no more."

• *How do you feel as you recall this passage from John 8?*

_____

_____

## Characteristics of the Gift of Exhortation

The gift of exhortation is characterized by the following eight principles:

1. *The person with a gift of exhortation desires to see others mature in their faith.* The exhorter desires to see that others are growing in their spiritual lives. Exhorters are people oriented, discipleship oriented, growth oriented, and maturity oriented. Read again what Paul said to the Colossians: "warning every man . . . that we may present every man perfect in Christ Jesus" (Col. 1:28).

The exhorter is quick to ask, "Where are you in your spiritual life? Are you growing? In what ways?"

- *In your life, have you been asked this question recently? How do you feel about hearing such a question asked of you? What was or is your response?*

———————————————————————

———————————————————————

2. *The person with a gift of exhortation desires to see others discover their spiritual potential.* The exhorter does not want another person to be anything less than what God has called him or her to be. The person with this gift usually can discern the potential of another person and can visualize his spiritual achievement. The exhorter has insight as to what God might do in and through a person if that person yielded all of his or her talents, abilities, and energy to the Lord.

Once an exhorter sees your potential, the exhorter feels compelled to encourage you to reach your potential and to turn away from anything that detracts from or might diminish your growth in Christ.

3. *The person with a gift of exhortation is quick to ask questions about a person's general welfare, often in an attempt to discover the individual's spiritual welfare.* The exhorter will do his utmost to find a way of communicating with another person. The

exhorter is "other oriented"—he will ask questions and probe until he is satisfied that the person is growing in Christ Jesus. If he discovers an error or blockage in another's growth, he will be quick to point it out and to identify the steps that need to be taken for the person to get back on track with the Lord or to continue to grow.

Paul never hesitated to say to others, "I have heard *this* about you," and then Paul always went on to give God's wisdom for how the problem should be resolved.

To the person who is choosing sin, who is in rebellion, or who is apathetic toward growing spiritually, the exhorter may seem to be too aggressive or too "personal." The person who comes face to face with exhortation may feel as if he is on the hot seat. The exhorter, however, if he or she is truly following the leading of the Holy Spirit, is not desirous of producing guilt or shame. Rather, he wants to know and help the other person move forward in a personal relationship with the Lord.

A number of people with this gift seem to gravitate toward a career in counseling. They are people who want to see others grow, develop, and become sound in their faith.

• *Have you ever been "confronted" by an exhorter? How did you feel? What did they say? What was your response? What was the result?*

_____

_____

• *Have you ever exhorted another person? How did you feel as you engaged in exhortation? What did you say? What was the response? What was the result?*

_____

_____

4. *The godly exhorter must always point others toward Christ Jesus.* The truth of God's Word and the truth of Jesus Christ's

life and death on the cross must always be central to exhortation. Otherwise, the exhorter is only giving human advice and human wisdom. Truly to be operating with the spiritual motivational gift of exhortation, the exhorter must identify ways in which a person can and must turn *to* Christ and *to* the Holy Spirit, following Jesus Christ as his example and trusting in the Holy Spirit for daily guidance. This is true not only for the exhorter, of course, but for any person who wants to be an effective witness for Jesus Christ. Paul's entire theme for the churches was this: "Christ Jesus in me, and I in Christ Jesus."

• *In what ways are you feeling challenged in your spirit?*

_____

_____

5. *The gift of exhortation includes the ability to give precise instructions about how a person might grow in relationship with Christ.* Those with this gift have an ability to understand precisely what is necessary for people to make corrections in their lives and move forward without hindrances. Exhorters are "step one, step two, step three" people. They understand the steps necessary for people to apply the truth of God's Word to their lives. Throughout his letters, Paul writes step-by-step instructions for the believers to mature in their faith. His arguments for the faith are well organized and completely thought through so that those who read his admonitions understand clearly what Paul is saying and desiring on their behalf.

6. *The person with the gift of exhortation has learned value in suffering.* The exhorter desires to see a person avoid suffering and to come through suffering victoriously, but the godly exhorter also has learned that suffering can have great value in a person's life in breaking old patterns of sin and in causing adoption of new patterns of right behavior. Paul learned the lessons associated with suffering. He wrote to the Corinthians, "He [Christ Jesus] said to me, 'My grace is sufficient for you,

for My strength is made perfect in weakness.' Therefore most gladly I will rather boast in my infirmities, that the power of Christ may rest upon me. Therefore I take pleasure in infirmities, in reproaches, in needs, in persecutions, in distresses, for Christ's sake. For when I am weak, then I am strong" (2 Cor. 12:9–10).

The person who exhorts may not appear to be very sympathetic with the person who is struggling or suffering because the exhorter is so concerned with the person beginning to take steps to grow and to make changes to get out of repetitive struggling and suffering. The person who exhorts must exhort with compassion.

7. *The gift of exhortation is concerned with the application of God's Word.* The prophet wants to make sure the truth is proclaimed; the teacher wants to make sure that it is the whole truth and nothing but the truth that is taught. The exhorter asks, "How can this be applied to life? What should a person do with this truth?" Paul is always concerned with *how* a person is to follow Christ and *what* a person must do to manifest godly behavior and grow in faith.

The teacher begins with the Word of God and then presents it as opportunities arise. The exhorter looks at the needs of people, then to the Word of God for answers, returning to people with the application of God's Word for them.

8. *Those with a gift of exhortation want to be with people and "see" firsthand how they are growing in their faith.* Exhorters are usually very good at reading body language and facial expressions. Paul wrote again and again to the churches, "I long to be with you," "I can hardly wait to see you again," "I was so grateful to hear about you from someone who recently was with you."

One of the chief concerns of those who exhort is to resolve conflicts among groups of people. The person with a gift of exhortation does not shy away from relational problems, but seeks to get right in the middle to help sort them out and bring healing and reconciliation. Paul's writings often focus on how people should relate to one another, including husbands and wives, parents and children, slaves and slave owners, Jews and Greeks, "bonded" and "free." Paul is always concerned with the establishment of unity in the Body of Christ.

The person with this gift delights in being around people who are very interested in deepening their spiritual lives. He often has little patience with those who want only to live superficially.

- *What new insights do you have into the gift of exhortation?*

---

---

| What the Word Says | What the Word Says to Me |
|---|---|
| And when they had preached the gospel to that city and made many disciples, they returned to Lystra, Iconium, and Antioch, strengthening the souls of the disciples, exhorting them to continue in the faith, and saying, "We must through many tribulations enter the kingdom of God." (Acts 14:21–22) | ------------------------------ ------------------------------ ------------------------------ ------------------------------ ------------------------------ ------------------------------ ------------------------------ ------------------------------ ------------------------------ ------------------------------ |
| When he came and had seen the grace of God, he was glad, and encouraged them all that with purpose of heart they should continue with the Lord. (Acts 11:23) | ------------------------------ ------------------------------ ------------------------------ ------------------------------ ------------------------------ |
| I have written to you briefly, exhorting and testifying that | ------------------------------ ------------------------------ |

this is the true grace of God in which you stand. (1 Peter 5:12)

For our exhortation did not come from error or uncleanness, nor was it in deceit. But as we have been approved by God to be entrusted with the gospel, even so we speak, not as pleasing men, but God who tests our hearts. For neither at any time did we use flattering words, as you know, nor a cloak for covetousness—God is witness. Nor did we seek glory from men, either from you or from others, when we might have made demands as apostles of Christ. But we were gentle among you, just as a nursing mother cherishes her own children. So, affectionately longing for you, we were well pleased to impart to you not only the gospel of God, but also our own lives, because you had become dear to us. (1 Thess. 2:3–8)

- *In your life, cite several examples of those who have genuinely encouraged you in your walk with Christ. How did they manifest their encouragement?*

## Words of Caution to Those Who Exhort

The person with the gift of exhortation must be cautious in these areas:

*The exhorter must not oversimplify a problem to the person experiencing the problem.* He must not promise solutions too quickly or give a "quick-fix" formula. If he does, the person with the need is likely to reject the wisdom, believing it is too simplistic a solution for a great need. This is not to say that the solution offered is wrong. Rather, the exhorter must deal with others in compassion and lead the person in need through the steps required, one by one.

*The exhorter must be able to empathize.* He must seek to identify as fully as possible with the person in need. He must try to feel what they feel and see what they see. The world through their eyes in order to understand more fully how to help them feel differently and see the truth with greater clarity.

*The exhorter must not lose sight of the importance of leading people to Christ Jesus.* Exhorters are primarily concerned with the growth and maturity of those who are believers. They may be perceived as being unconcerned about the lost. Exhorters can be excellent evangelists and witnesses for Christ if they will see their ministries in broader terms of leading people from darkness to light.

*The exhorter must be skilled in applying the Word of God within the context of the Scriptures as a whole.* At times, those who exhort are so quick to apply the Scriptures that they may be tempted to lift a single verse out of context and offer it as a solution. Now, the Bible is as applicable to our lives today as it was to those for whom it was first written. The exhorter must look for meaning and application that spans all cultures and all history. He must see the entire scope of God's truth.

What is true for an exhorter, of course, is true for all Christians. We each must become skilled in applying the *whole* of God's Word to our lives, in winning others to Christ, and in leading people from where they are to where God desires for them to be. The exhorter is one who is *gifted* in a special way by the Holy Spirit to do this intuitively and responsively.

• *In what ways are you challenged in your spirit?*

_____

_____

## Many Exhorters in the Church

We have noted in previous lessons that few within the church are given the ministry gifts of prophecy and teaching. In contrast, many are given the gift of service. *Many* are also given the gift of exhortation. The church needs many who will exhort and encourage others to reach their potential in Christ.

Each person needs to have at least one person who functions in the role of an exhorter in his or her life. This is a person who asks periodically, and sincerely, "What is God doing in your life? What are you doing to develop your relationship with the Lord? In what ways is the Lord working in your life to make you more like Christ Jesus?"

• *In your walk with Christ, do you have a person who functions as an exhorter to you?*

_____

_____

| What the Word Says | What the Word Says to Me |
|---|---|
| Let us hold fast the confession of our hope without wavering, for He who promised is faithful. And let us consider one another in order to stir up love and good works, not forsaking | ------------------------------ <br> ------------------------------ <br> ------------------------------ <br> ------------------------------ <br> ------------------------------ <br> ------------------------------ |

the assembling of ourselves together, as is the manner of some, but exhorting one another, and so much the more as you see the Day approaching. (Heb. 10:23–25)

-----------------------------
-----------------------------
-----------------------------
-----------------------------
-----------------------------
-----------------------------

Beware, brethren, lest there be in any of you an evil heart of unbelief in departing from the living God; but exhort one another daily, while it is called "Today," lest any of you be hardened through the deceitfulness of sin. (Heb. 3:12–13)

-----------------------------
-----------------------------
-----------------------------
-----------------------------
-----------------------------
-----------------------------
-----------------------------

Now I myself am confident concerning you, my brethren, that you also are full of goodness, filled with all knowledge, able also to admonish one another. (Rom. 15:14)

-----------------------------
-----------------------------
-----------------------------
-----------------------------
-----------------------------
-----------------------------

The person you seek to have as an exhorter must be a person who will exemplify this behavior:

- *Wisdom*—to understand the Word of God and how it might be applied to you
- *Discernment*—to be able to "slice open mentally and see the truth for what it is," to see clearly your spirit and your potential
- *Faith*—to believe God can take you from where you are to where He desires you to be
- *Discretion*—to keep what he knows about you in confidence

and to lead you step by step into the greater future God has for you

- *Love*—to desire the best in your life and always be willing to give you his best, offering you God's truth without personal judgment or condemnation
- *Creative*—to recognize that you are a unique individual and God's Word must be applied to your life creatively at any particular moment and in light of particular circumstances
- *Enthusiasm*—to be able to inspire you to desire more in your Christian walk

If you allow a person with these qualities to help you as he or she receives guidance from the Holy Spirit, you will be greatly blessed! Ask the Lord Jesus Christ to lead you to such a person.

- *What new insights do you have into the gift of exhortation?*

  _____

  _____

- *In what ways are you feeling challenged in your spirit?*

  _____

  _____

# LESSON 7

# THE GIFT OF GIVING

Do you respond immediately to the presence of a need by saying, "What can I do? How can I help solve this need?" You may be a person who has been given the gift of giving.

A person in the Bible who exemplifies the gift of giving is Matthew. There are several reasons I believe Matthew had this gift. First, he has more to say in general about giving than any other New Testament writer. Second, he offers more wise counsel about giving, and he is the only one who makes the statement that our giving should be done in "secret." And third, he is the one who addresses the issue of *misuse* of money and resources.

Matthew was a tax collector, so he was familiar with money and financial transactions. He is the Gospel writer who knows from personal experience a great deal about money and whether it is being used righteously or unrighteously. Matthew is the one who gives us the details about the gifts brought to Jesus. He is the one who records Jesus' condemnation of the Pharisees for allowing people to avoid caring for their parents financially, and who tells us about what the Pharisees did with the thirty pieces of silver that Judas returned to them after he had betrayed Jesus. As you look at the Gospel of Matthew, you will find a great deal of information about money, finances, material possessions, and the proper use of our resources.

At the outset of our discussion about giving, let me make three general statements about giving.

1. *We are to give regardless of our situation in life.* Giving is not a ministry or motivational gift that is limited to those who are wealthy. A person's financial status has nothing to do with the motivational gift of giving. The person with this gift will *desire* to give regardless of the size of his bank account or the amount of possessions he has; the person with this gift will delight in giving and will find great satisfaction in giving.

2. *All of us are commanded to give, and to do so with liberality.* We are to give our tithes faithfully and be generous in our offerings. The person with the gift of giving, however, is a person who "lives to give." This person can't help but give at every opportunity—he is always alert to opportunities to give and quick to give as much as he can as often as he can. We must never leave the giving to those who have this gift. Each of us is to give as God commands.

3. *Giving is not limited to money.* A gift may be one of material resources, time, talent, energy, or creativity. The gift, however, will be one that has *value*, and which produces or conveys a *material benefit.* The giver may volunteer time and talent and energy to a particular cause, knowing that his or her effort will produce a tangible or material blessing to others. Again, we all are to give in a multitude of ways, but the person with the motivational gift of giving is a person who is eager to give in every way possible. He or she "can't help but give."

• *Do you know someone who has this motivational gift? Have you been given the ministry gift of giving?*

_____

_____

## Characteristics of the Gift of Giving

The ministry gift of giving has the following ten distinct characteristics:

1. *The person with a motivational gift of giving generally has a keen ability to make wise investments and purchases in order to have more money to give.* Many people are bargain hunters and wise investors. The person with the gift of giving, however, seeks to save and to invest *in order to have more to give.* Many bargain hunters desire to save money so they can spend the savings on themselves; the person who is a "giver" desires to spend the savings on the work of the Lord.

Read the parable that Jesus taught in Matthew 25:14–30, and note especially verse 29: "For to everyone who has, more will be given, and he will have abundance."

- *How do you feel about "extra" money that you may have?*

_____

_____

2. *The person with the gift of giving has a desire to give quietly so not to call attention to himself.* Persons with a gift of giving are not motivated by applause or public recognition. They find their satisfaction in making the gift. In fact, their total emphasis is on meeting the need, not on having others acknowledge that they have met the need.

Matthew recorded this teaching of Jesus:

[Jesus taught], "Take heed that you do not do your charitable deeds before men, to be seen by them. Otherwise you have no reward from your Father in heaven. Therefore, when you do a charitable deed, do not sound a trumpet before you as the hypocrites do in the synagogues and in the streets, that they may have glory from men. Assuredly, I say to you, they have their reward. But when you do a charitable deed, do not let your left hand know what your right hand is doing, that your charitable deed may be in secret, and your Father who sees in secret will Himself reward you openly." (Matt. 6:1–4)

3. *Those with this gift often do not respond to great pressure to give or to ardent appeals by professional fund-raisers.* They want to give out of their own inner motivation, not from outward pressure. They are turned off by high-pressure tactics. They often respond readily, however, to simple requests from those who obviously are in need.

Again, it is Matthew who recorded these words of Jesus: "Give to him who asks you, and from him who wants to borrow from you do not turn away" (Matt. 5:42).

• *How do you feel when you read Matthew 5:42?*

_____

_____

4. *The person with the gift of giving is usually eager to motivate others to give.* The person desires so greatly that a need be met that he will challenge others around him—regardless of their financial situation—to give what they can. The person also knows the value of giving, that there is a cycle to giving that includes receiving. The giving-receiving-giving-receiving cycle is motivating and rewarding, and the person with the gift of giving knows this cycle personally and desires that others experience it.

| What the Word Says | What the Word Says to Me |
|---|---|
| Give, and it will be given to you: good measure, pressed down, shaken together, and running over will be put into your bosom. For with the same measure that you use, it will be | _____ _____ _____ _____ _____ _____ |

measured back to you. (Luke
6:38)

He who sows sparingly will
also reap sparingly, and he who
sows bountifully will also reap
bountifully. (2 Cor. 9:6)

    • *In what ways are you challenged in your spirit by Luke
      6:38?*

   5. *The person with the gift of giving often has an ability to see
financial and material needs that others overlook.* He is quick to
calculate how much is needed, when it will be needed, and
how resources might best be applied to meeting the need.
   6. *The person with the gift of giving often judges others on the
basis of their giving.* He regards stewardship over material possessions and finances as being indicative of a person's ability
to be a good steward of spiritual matters. He takes to heart the
teaching of Jesus:

> He who is faithful in what is least is faithful also in
> much; and he who is unjust in what is least is unjust also
> in much. Therefore if you have not been faithful in the
> unrighteous mammon [money], who will commit to
> your trust the true riches? And if you have not been
> faithful in what is another man's, who will give you what
> is your own? (Luke 16:10–12)

   Because givers are very concerned about good stewardship,
they may live frugally and modestly, even though they have
great financial wealth. Generous givers are often unrecognized
because they are unpretentious in what they possess and use.

They are not motivated to accumulate things, but rather to use things to benefit others. They desire to gain wealth only so they can give away as much as possible in their lifetime.

- *What new insights do you have into the motivational gift of giving?*

_____

_____

7. *The person with the gift of giving rejoices when he perceives that his giving is an answer to someone else's prayer.* Those with this gift delight in being the tools that the Lord has used. They rejoice because they have added assurance that they heard correctly from the Lord. They rejoice that a legitimate need has been met. They rejoice that the faith of another person has been activated and built up. The person with a gift of giving always wants to be right on target when it comes to sensing needs and responding as the Lord leads.

8. *The person with the gift of giving relies upon the wise counsel of his spouse.* Those with this gift are so concerned about being good stewards that they look for confirmation that they are acting in obedience to the Lord. If the Lord is dealing with one godly person about making a gift to meet a need, He will deal likewise godly spouse about the gift.

9. *The person with the gift of giving desires to give gifts of high quality.* He or she does not look for the cheapest or most meager way to meet a need. Rather, the giver wants to give in abundance and quality, just as he perceives the Lord has given to him in abundance and quality.

10. *Persons with the gift of giving take joy in being a part of the ministry of the person to whom they have given.* When a giver makes a material gift, he feels as if he is giving part of himself. He feels "personally invested" in the ministry or the life of the person to which he has given. Being part of another person's success brings the giver joy.

| What the Word Says | What the Word Says to Me |
|---|---|
| So let each one give as he purposes in his heart, not grudgingly or of necessity; for God loves a cheerful giver. And God is able to make all grace abound toward you, that you, always having all sufficiency in all things, may have an abundance for every good work. (2 Cor. 9:7) | -------------------------------<br>-------------------------------<br>-------------------------------<br>-------------------------------<br>-------------------------------<br>-------------------------------<br>-------------------------------<br>-------------------------------<br>-------------------------------<br>------------------------------- |

## Words of Caution to the Giver

Givers must guard against these tendencies:

- *They must never become so overly concerned with material goods that they neglect the spiritual dimension of their lives.*
- *They must never attempt to control the work of a ministry or the life of another person through their financial or material gifts.* At times, those who give are concerned with making certain that their gift is used in a proper way. Those who give must "release" their gifts to the work of God and trust others to manage and administer the gifts they give.
- *They must never pressure others to give as generously as they do.* Just as the people with this gift often reject high-pressure tactics, so they must be careful not to engage in high-pressure tactics themselves.
- *They must never become stingy to their own families.* Those who are intensely concerned about the needs of others often overlook the needs of their spouses and children. Legitimate needs of family members should be met.
- *They must always remember to be thankful for what they receive.* Givers are often so focused on their own giving

that they either rebuff or fail to acknowledge properly the
things they are given by others.

| What the Word Says | What the Word Says to Me |
|---|---|
| For what will it profit a man if he gains the whole world, and loses his own soul? Or what will a man give in exchange for his soul? (Mark 8:36–37) | _____ |
| I rejoiced in the Lord greatly that now at last your care for me has flourished again; though you surely did care, but you lacked opportunity . . . not that I seek the gift, but I seek the fruit that abounds to your account. (Phil. 4:10,17) | _____ |

## The Behaviors of the Godly Giver

Those persons who truly are motivated by the Holy Spirit
to manifest the gift of giving will be known by these characteristics:

- *Thrifty*—they will spend their money wisely, not wasting money that could otherwise be used for ministry purposes
- *Resourceful*—they will find a way to see a need met, either through their own giving or by motivating the giving of others
- *Contented*—they will be content with what they have
- *Punctual*—they recognize that it is better to meet a need quickly than to allow a need to grow into an even greater need that will require even greater resources to meet
- *Tolerant*—they can often "give and take" in areas where others sometimes find it difficult to be flexible

- *Cautious*—they often research carefully their investments, and the ministries to which they give so that they are certain to use their resources wisely
- *Thankful*—they appreciate what they have and are grateful when they are used by God to meet a need

  - *In your life, have you met a person who manifested these behaviors in the way they gave to you personally or to your church or a ministry in which you are involved? How did this person encourage you to become a more generous giver?*

    _____

    _____

  - *In what ways are you feeling challenged in your spirit?*

    _____

    _____

## What the Word Says

[Jesus taught], "Freely you have received, freely give." (Matt. 10:8)

In everything give thanks; for this is the will of God in Christ Jesus for you. (1 Thess. 5:18)

Command those who are rich in this present age not to be haughty, nor to trust in uncertain riches but in the living God, who gives us richly all things to enjoy. Let them do good, that they be rich in good works, ready to give, willing to share, storing up for

## What the Word Says to Me

_____

_____

_____

_____

_____

_____

_____

_____

_____

_____

_____

_____

_____

themselves a good foundation
for the time to come, that they
may lay hold on eternal life.
(1 Tim. 6:17–19)

------------------------------

------------------------------

------------------------------

------------------------------

[Jesus said], "For where your
treasure is, there your heart
will be also." (Luke 12:34)

------------------------------

------------------------------

------------------------------

## Jesus—Our Role Model for Giving

Jesus, of course, is our role model for sacrificial, joyful, and purposeful giving. No person has ever given as Jesus gave, for He gave His very life on the cross so that you and I might have eternal life. Jesus taught His disciples: "Greater love has no one than this, than to lay down one's life for his friends" (John 15:13). Jesus willingly gave His life in obedience to His father. Perhaps the most famous verse in the entire New Testament is a verse about giving: "For God so loved the world that He gave His only begotten Son, that whoever believes in Him should not perish but have everlasting life" (John 3:16).

The person who has the motivational gift of giving has a tremendous opportunity to be a blessing to others in the Body of Christ, to encourage others in the proper use of their finances, and to make the extension of the gospel possible.

- *What new insights do you have into the motivational gift of giving?*

  _____

  _____

- *In what ways are you feeling challenged in your spirit?*

  _____

  _____

# LESSON 8

# THE GIFT OF ORGANIZATION

Are you uncomfortable in a "leaderless" group? Do you feel restless or frustrated if things seem to be disorderly? You may be a person who has been given the motivational gift of organization.

This gift is sometimes called the gift of leading, ruling, or the gift of administration. The Greek word literally means "the one who stands out front."

The person who has the gift of organization is frequently misunderstood. Often, this gift is not perceived as being very spiritual, or it is perceived as being a matter solely of human will. We must never lose sight that God, our heavenly Father, created the universe, including us human beings, with a strong sense of order. God created in a very precise, sequential, and organized manner. The laws of nature and of human nature are extremely practical in their application, and yet they are unseen laws. Issues of authority and rulership are deeply rooted in the spiritual realm. And last but not least, the church was designed by God to function with order, with all gifts of the Holy Spirit exercised in an orderly way.

The person with the gift of organization is no less spiritual than those who bear any of the other ministry gifts. In fact, to the Christian all things are spiritual. There is no distinction before God between secular life and spiritual life—*all* of life is spiritual. Everything has a spiritual foundation. The person who is given the motivational gift of organization is one who is given a degree of insight into what God is doing and desires to be done. The person with this gift might be called a "spiritual dreamer in action"—a person who can see the intended design of God and turn it into reality. He or she has the capacity to see what God is doing in the spiritual realm, how God desires to bring about spiritual results in the physical realm, and understands immediately how to engage in a major undertaking to turn the will of God into a reality on this earth. He has an ability to visualize the final result God desires.

A person in the New Testament who exhibits the ministry gift of organization is James. One of the main criticisms of James is that he is too practical and not spiritual enough—he emphasizes works as being of equal importance to faith. Now, we must not misunderstand James. He regards faith very highly and sees no substitute for faith. But, he is very concerned that faith be put to *work* in an orderly and effective way.

- *Do you know someone who has the ministry gift of organization? Is this the motivational gift that has been given to you?*

  _____

  _____

## Orderly and Effective Works

Throughout the epistle of James we find a strong admonition that we be "doers of the word and not hearers only" (James 1:22). In fact, James says that if we are hearers and believers only, and not doers, we have deceived ourselves. As you read through the verses from James below, note his great practical concern for orderliness and diligence.

| What the Word Says | What the Word Says to Me |
|---|---|
| If anyone is a hearer of the word and not a doer, he is like | ------------------------------- ------------------------------- |

a man observing his natural face in a mirror; for he observes himself, goes away, and immediately forgets what kind of man he was. But he who looks into the perfect law of liberty and continues in it, and is not a forgetful hearer but a doer of the work, this one will be blessed in what he does. (James 1:23–25)

Pure and undefiled religion before God and the Father is this: to visit orphans and widows in their trouble, and to keep oneself unspotted from the world. (James 1:27)

If a brother or sister is naked and destitute of daily food, and one of you says to him, "Depart in peace, be warmed and filled," but you do not give them the things which are needed for the body, what does it profit? Thus also faith by itself, if it does not have works, is dead. (James 2:15–17)

Who is wise and understanding among you? Let him show by good conduct that his works are done in the meekness of wisdom. (James 3:13)

For where envy and self-
seeking exist, confusion and
every evil thing are there. But
the wisdom that is from above
is first pure, then peaceable,
gentle, willing to yield, full of
mercy and good fruits, without
partiality, and without
hypocrisy. (James 3:16–17)

To him who knows to do good
and does not do it, to him it is
sin. (James 4:17)

- *In what ways are you feeling challenged in your spirit?*

## A Picture of Order in the Early Church

James was the leader of the church in Jerusalem—as some
have said, the "first church." Early in the formation of the
church, problems arose in the distribution of food. Many of the
believers had pooled their earthly resources and were meeting
together daily for fellowship, for study of the Word, and for eat-
ing meals. Some were being neglected while others were
indulging themselves. As you read below what happened, note
how organization was linked to spiritual concerns and how organization created a climate in which spiritual fruit was produced.

Then the twelve summoned the multitude of the disciples and said, "It is not desirable that we should leave
the word of God and serve tables. Therefore, brethren,
seek out from among you seven men of good reputa-
tion, full of the Holy Spirit and wisdom, whom we may
appoint over this business; but we will give ourselves
continually to prayer and to the ministry of the word."

And the saying pleased the whole multitude. And they chose Stephen, a man full of faith and the Holy Spirit, and Philip, Prochorus, Nicanor, Timon, Parmenas, and Nicolas, a proselyte from Antioch, whom they set before the apostles; and when they had prayed, they laid hands on them.

Then the word of God spread, and the number of the disciples multiplied greatly in Jerusalem, and a great many of the priests were obedient to the faith. (Acts 6:2–7)

Organization is not counterproductive to the work of the Holy Spirit in a group. Rather, the Holy Spirit desires order. When the ministry gift of organization is strong and Spirit-led in a group, all other ministry gifts flourish. The gospel is preached, souls are saved, and the church grows and develops even greater strength.

• *What new insights do you have into Acts 6:2–7?*

_____

_____

## Characteristics of the Gift of Organization

The person who has the gift of organization bears the following twelve characteristics.

1. *Those with the gift of organization have an ability to see the "big picture."* They have a capacity to dream big and to believe that God desires to do "something more" than presently exists.
2. *Those with the gift of organization have an ability to break down large projects into bite-sized pieces.* They are able to break down long-range goals into a sequence of short-range goals.

3. *Those with the gift of organization are self-starters.* They are highly motivated to accomplish the goals that are before them. They take great joy in seeing the pieces of the larger puzzle fall into place one by one.

4. *Those with the gift of organization are keenly aware of all the resources necessary for accomplishing a goal.* The minute this person sees the goal that God sets before him, he begins to analyze all that is necessary for accomplishing the goal, and begins to envision ways that the necessary resources might be acquired.

   • *In your life, have you had an experience in which you were part of a group that was led ably by a godly person with the gift of organization?*

   _____

   _____

   • *Have you had an experience in which you were in a group that was* not *led by a skilled and godly leader?*

   _____

   _____

5. *Those with the gift of organization are very positive that God-given goals can be accomplished.* They are can-do people, and they have very little tolerance for those with objections, unfounded concerns, and a negative or pessimistic outlook.

6. *Those with the gift of organization know how to delegate.* They know they can't do it all, and they are willing to relinquish both authority and responsibility so that others can be successful in undertaking and completing part of the larger goal. They know how to seek out the right people to undertake various parts of the task that lies ahead.

7. *Those with the gift of organization often have little tolerance for details.* Too many details can bog down the person who has the gift of organization.

8. *Those with the gift of organization have a capacity to receive criticism without crumbling.* As mentioned earlier, the literal meaning of the Greek word for ruling or leading is "the one who stands out front." The person who is out front is on the firing line—he is the one most likely to be criticized, questioned, blamed, misunderstood, and to face arguments. He *has* to have skin as thick as a rhinoceros. If he is to accomplish God's plan, he must not allow criticism to deter him or slow him down.

9. *The person with the gift of organization has a need to know that those with whom he is working are loyal to him and committed to the task at hand.* The person who leads expects loyalty, not only to himself, but to God. The person with this gift is so loyal to God and so committed to obeying God that he has little tolerance for any person who is disloyal or wavering in commitment.

10. *Those with the gift of organization have a tendency to move into a leadership role if no leader emerges or if a situation becomes disorderly.* They cannot sit idly on the sidelines if they perceive that nobody is moving into a leadership role. Because of this tendency the person with this gift can sometimes be misinterpreted as being egotistical or too aggressive. In fact, the person is simply moving to establish order where he perceives disorder.

   • *How do you feel when a group is without a strong leader or a focused direction?*

   _____

   _____

11. *Those with the gift of organization want to see a goal reached as quickly as possible, as well as possible, and with as few resources as possible.* They abhor wasted time, wasted money, wasted talent, wasted resources, and wasted energy.

12. *Those with the gift of organization delight in seeing projects accomplished.* They are not motivated by making money, working with people, or receiving applause for the finished job—rather, they are motivated by seeing the task accomplished in a way they believe is pleasing to God. They need few rewards other than the deep satisfaction they feel that God is pleased and that good work has been done.

• *What new insights do you have into the ministry gift of organization?*

_____

_____

| What the Word Says | What the Word Says to Me |
|---|---|
| Having then gifts differing according to the grace that is given to us, let us use them . . . he who leads, with diligence. (Rom. 12:6, 8) | |
| Let all things be done decently and in order. (1 Cor. 14:40) | |
| For the administration of this service not only supplies the needs of the saints, but also is abounding through many thanksgivings to God. (2 Cor. 9:12) | |

• *In what ways are you feeling challenged in your spirit?*

_____

_____

## Warnings to Those with the Gift of Organization

The person who has the motivational gift of organization must be aware of these negative tendencies:

- *Never taking time to rest or reflect.* Those with this gift are rarely without a project to do. As soon as they complete one project they are eager to move on to the next one. None of us was created to be all work and no play. God made the Sabbath for man to rest physically, emotionally, and spiritually—to relax in His presence and allow God to rejuvenate us from the inside out.

- *Driving others beyond the limits of their abilities.* The person with a gift of organization is so highly motivated to complete a task that he or she may "drive" others to work without regard for their capacity, energy level, other commitments, or personal limitations. They must be sensitive to the fact that others may not be as talented, motivated, energetic, focused, or insightful as they are.

- *Relying on their own abilities rather than trusting God to guide the setting of priorities.* Those with this motivational gift are usually so capable that they must guard against the tendency to run ahead of God's timetable or to fail to ask God often, "Are we doing what You want us to do? Are we doing this in the way You want us to do it? Do we have our priorities straight?"

| What the Word Says | What the Word Says to Me |
|---|---|
| Come now, you who say, "Today or tomorrow we will go to such and such a city, spend a year there, buy and sell, and make a profit"; whereas you do not know what will happen tomorrow. For what is your | ----------------------------- <br> ----------------------------- <br> ----------------------------- <br> ----------------------------- <br> ----------------------------- <br> ----------------------------- <br> ----------------------------- |

life? It is even a vapor that
appears for a little time and
then vanishes away. Instead
you ought to say, "If the Lord
wills, we shall live and do this
or that." (James 4:13–15)

----------------------------------
----------------------------------
----------------------------------
----------------------------------
----------------------------------
----------------------------------

• *In what ways are you feeling challenged in your spirit?*

_____

_____

## Behavior of the Godly Administrator

If you have been placed into an administrative or leadership role, seek to develop the qualities of behavior listed below. If you are seeking to work effectively for a godly administrator or leader, look for these qualities to be manifested in a consistent manner:

- *Orderliness*—every aspect of life is subject to order
- *Initiative*—no delay in taking action
- *Responsibility*—willing to take responsibility for all aspects of a project or group endeavor
- *Humility*—a recognition that others must be part of the team if the job is to be done quickly and effectively; neither domineering nor dictatorial
- *Decisiveness*—able to make a decision quickly even in the face of criticism
- *Determination*—knowing the goal is worthy of the price that must be paid for the job to get done
- *Loyalty*—to God and to others in authority, as well as loyal to those who are following his leadership

Such a godly leader, who regards himself to be under the authority of the Holy Spirit, is a joy to work with and for! An ungodly leader is a tyrant to be avoided.

- *In your life, have you had the privilege of working for a godly leader who followed the guidance of the Holy Spirit? What were the results? How did you feel working for or with that person?*

_____

_____

## Jesus—The Head of the Church

Paul had this to say about Jesus as the One who orders all things in His church: "He put all things under His feet, and gave Him to be head over all things to the church, which is His body, the fullness of Him who fills all in all" (Eph. 1:22).

Jesus referred to Himself as the Shepherd of His flock. When it came to organizing His disciples, Jesus chose twelve to be apostles, and He sent His disciples out two by two. Jesus was certainly delegating authority when He gave His disciples this commandment: "Go into all the world and preach the gospel to every creature" (Mark 16:15). As with all of the ministry gifts, Jesus is our role model for the proper administration of the gift of organization.

We each are to be orderly in the way we conduct our lives. The people with this ministry gift, however, find great satisfaction in being organized and in seeing work done, tasks accomplished, and projects completed. They *enjoy* work and are likely to be working every day of their lives.

- *What new insights do you have into the ministry gift of organization?*

_____

_____

- *In what ways are you feeling challenged in your spirit?*

_____

_____

# LESSON 9

# THE GIFT OF MERCY

Do you have a real heart for people? Do you feel tenderness toward others? Are you concerned with finding ways of showing kindness? Do you have a desire to see people love one another to a greater degree? You are likely a person who has been given the gift of mercy.

One of the people who best exemplifies the gift of mercy in the New Testament is the apostle John. One of the foremost characteristics of the person gifted with mercy is love, and of all the apostles John is the one who wrote the most about love—the love of God, the commandments of Jesus to love one another, and extensive admonitions to the early believers about love. John valued love highly and often referred to himself as "the one whom Jesus loved." To have been loved by Jesus was the highest reward and the most meaningful mark of identification that John felt he could claim for himself.

Very often men seem to think that mercy is a feminine gift. It is neither feminine nor masculine. It is a character quality that every believer is to manifest. Very often the person who is gifted with mercy is the one who seems tough on the outside, but is very tenderhearted and kind on the inside. John was not the least bit effeminate—he was called by Jesus as a "son of thunder." Yet John was tenderhearted and merciful.

The person who bears this gift of mercy is the "joy" in any body of believers—he or she is the one everyone else enjoys having around and is eager to see. And we can readily understand why! Who is it that fails to respond to unconditional love and mercy?

- *Do you know someone who has the gift of mercy? Have you been given this motivational gift?*

_____

_____

## John's Focus on Love in the Church

John wrote a great deal about the need for love in the Body of Christ. As you read through the verses below, notice that John always saw love as an *active* word, not as an emotion only. He always related love to Jesus Christ, who truly is our source of love. Without Christ Jesus, it is impossible for a person truly to love unconditionally.

### What the Word Says

My little children, let us not love in word or in tongue, but in deed and in truth. (1 John 3:18)

This is His commandment: that we should believe on the name of His Son Jesus Christ and love one another, as He gave us commandment. (1 John 3:23)

Beloved, let us love one loved

### What the Word Says to Me

_____

_____

_____

_____

_____

_____

_____

_____

_____

_____

_____

another, for love is of God; and
everyone who loves is born of
God and knows God. He who
does not love does not know
God, for God is love. In this
the love of God was mani-
fested toward us, that God has
sent His only begotten Son
into the world, that we might
live through Him. In this is
love, not that we loved God,
but that He loved us and sent
His son to be the propitiation
for our sins. Beloved, if God so
loved us, we also ought to love
one another. (1 John 4:7–11)

Love has been perfected
among us in this: that we may
have boldness in the day of
judgment. (1 John 4:17)

There is no fear in love; but
perfect love casts out fear,
because fear involves torment.
(1 John 4:18)

We love Him because He first
loved us. (1 John 4:19)

If someone says, "I love God,"
and hates his brother, he is a
liar; for he who does not love
his brother whom he has seen,
how can he love God whom
he has not seen? And this

commandment we have from
Him: that he who loves God
must love his brother also.
(1 John 4:20–21)

--------------------------------
--------------------------------
--------------------------------
--------------------------------

## Characteristics of the Gift of Mercy

The motivational gift of mercy has a number of outstanding qualities, including these seven characteristics:

1. *Those with the gift of mercy have a great ability to feel the joy or distress of another person or a group.* They have a heightened sense of discernment regarding emotions. They rarely have to ask, "How are you doing?"—intuitively sensing how another person is doing emotionally. They are usually more concerned with inner hurts than with outer material or physical needs. They are especially drawn to those who are lonely, fearful, or troubled.

2. *Those with a gift of mercy are able to identify with others and to vicariously experience what others are going through.* They have a special empathy and understanding of those who are under emotional stress and are actively attracted to those individuals. They have a great hope and desire to be able to help others by their presence and friendship. They can "rejoice with those who rejoice, and weep with those who weep" (Rom. 12:15).

3. *Those with a gift of mercy desire to see those who are hurting alleviated of their hurt.* They see virtually no benefit in pain, suffering, distress, or sorrow. They want to see all negative feelings healed and removed immediately. At times they may clash with those who have the gift of exhortation, who are able to see benefit in suffering. The person who has the gift of mercy must be willing to allow the gift of exhortation to function fully, just as the person with the gift of exhortation must be patient and kind toward the person who has a gift of mercy. While

those with other ministry gifts may reach out to hurting individuals with words and material blessing, the person with the gift of mercy is likely to reach out with open arms.

4. *Those with the gift of mercy are very sensitive to statements and actions that may hurt others.* They intuitively feel pain on the behalf of others. They often react harshly if their friends or family members are rejected or hurt in any way. They may respond in a defensive and even angry way if they sense that a person is doing something that may injure emotionally a person they love. They are very sensitive to criticism of others.

5. *Those with the gift of mercy have an ability to sense genuine unconditional love and to detect expressions of love that are insincere or hypocritical.* They have a greater ability to be wounded themselves; they are highly vulnerable to feeling emotional pain. Part of the merciful person's ability to empathize with another person's emotional pain is the person's own inner awareness of, and past personal experience with emotional pain.

6. *Those with a gift of mercy have a great need for friendship.* They need to be in relationships that are marked by commitment and steadfastness. They do not have a high tolerance, however, for friends who manifest a critical spirit.

7. *Those with the gift of mercy are reluctant to speak against any person, regardless of what they have done.* The danger, of course, is that they may not speak up in times when they *should* confront evil. Mercy must always be balanced with justice. God is always merciful, but it is equally true that God is always just.

• *How do you feel about those who show mercy to you?*

_____

_____

## What the Word Says

Love your enemies, do good,
and lend, hoping for nothing
in return; and your reward will
be great, and you will be sons
of the Most High. For He is
kind to the unthankful and
evil. Therefore be merciful, just
as your Father also is merciful.
(Luke 6:35–36)

[Jesus said], "Blessed are the
merciful, for they shall obtain
mercy." (Matt. 5:7)

Having then gifts differing
according to the grace that is
given to us, let us use them . . .
he who shows mercy, with
cheerfulness. (Rom. 12:6, 8)

Therefore, as the elect of God,
holy and beloved, put on tender mercies, kindness,
humility, meekness, longsuffering; bearing with one another,
and forgiving one another, if
anyone has a complaint against
another; even as Christ forgave
you, so you also must do. But
above all these things put on
love, which is the bond of per-
fection. (Col. 3:12–14)

Be kind to one another, tender-

## What the Word Says to Me

------------------------------
------------------------------
------------------------------
------------------------------
------------------------------
------------------------------
------------------------------
------------------------------
------------------------------

------------------------------
------------------------------
------------------------------

------------------------------
------------------------------
------------------------------
------------------------------
------------------------------

------------------------------
------------------------------
------------------------------
------------------------------
------------------------------
------------------------------
------------------------------
------------------------------
------------------------------
------------------------------

------------------------------

hearted, forgiving one another,
even as God in Christ forgave
you. (Eph. 4:32)

-------------------------------
-------------------------------
-------------------------------

## Warnings to Those Gifted in Mercy

The person who is gifted in mercy must continually guard against these tendencies:

- *Being too emotional to the point of losing sight of the greater purposes of God.* The person with a gift of mercy must always maintain an objective awareness that God's purposes and God's methods are "higher" than those of men and women, and that God may at times "break" a person in order to refashion him.
- *Being weak and indecisive.* The person with this gift has a tendency to express tenderness and acceptance rather than firmness and resoluteness for the truth of God and righteous behavior. The merciful person must choose to stand strong in the face of evil.
- *Being too quick to draw conclusions in defense of those they believe are being criticized or hurt.* Those with this gift must not be too impulsive in showing mercy.
- *Being too forward in their desire to minister to others with their presence, forgiveness, and kindness.* Those with this gift must be sensitive to know when they are "too close" for another person's comfort.
- *Failing to note when acts of mercy and unconditional love cross an invisible line and become expressions of sexual desire.* Those with the gift of mercy are wise to extend their gift of mercy to those who are of the same sex. Because the gift of mercy is rooted in love, it is very difficult for some people to maintain proper bounds when showing mercy to those of the opposite sex. At times, those who receive mercy

from a person of the opposite sex misinterpret their acts of mercy as acts of romantic love.

• *In what ways are you feeling challenged in your spirit?*

_____

_____

## The Godly Expression of Mercy

The person with a gift of mercy who allows the Holy Spirit to guide him or her into acts of mercy is known by these traits:

- *Attentive*—watchful over those who are in need, sorrow, or trouble of any kind
- *Sensitive*—aware of the needs in others even without them saying anything
- *Fair*—desiring impartiality and fairness
- *Compassionate*—feeling the hurts of others as if they were their own
- *Gentle*—soft-spoken, tender, and caring
- *Yielding*—willing to give way to the desires and wishes of others so that harmony and peace might prevail in a person's heart
- *Sacrificial*—willing to suffer if it will help another person

As we have said for each of the motivational gifts, we each are to bear all fruits of the Spirit—one of the character traits identified as fruit in Galatians 5:22–23 is gentleness. The person who has the ministry gift of mercy is a person who does not have to say to himself or herself, "I should be merciful in this situation. I must speak kind words and deal with this person gently." Rather, the response of mercy and kindness is immediate, intuitive, and automatic. The person with this ministry gift actually seeks out those who are hurting so that he or she might show mercy. Nothing is as fulfilling to a person with this gift as having the opportunity to listen to, comfort, or dry the tears of another person who is hurting. Nothing is as important as defending the person who seems to be outcast, downtrodden, or treated unfairly.

- *Have you ever been the recipient of mercy from a person with the gift of mercy? How did you feel?*

_____

_____

## Jesus—Our Role Model for Mercy and Love

Jesus was the very embodiment of God's love—He was God's "only begotten son," sent to this world as an expression of God's infinite love for mankind. Jesus always acted in a merciful, loving way to people in need. He saw and responded to inner needs as much as to outer material or physical needs. His desire and goal was that mankind be reconciled to God the Father and experience God's forgiveness and unconditional love.

John wrote about Jesus and love: "By this we know love, because He laid down His life for us. And we also ought to lay down our lives for the brethren" (1 John 3:16).

John also wrote: "For God did not send His Son into the world to condemn the world, but that the world through Him might be saved" (John 3:17). Jesus did not merely talk about love or command others to love. He expressed love and gave love in the most generous and merciful way—He gave His very life for the sins of the world.

| What the Word Says | What the Word Says to Me |
|---|---|
| But God demonstrates His own love toward us, in that while we were still sinners, Christ died for us. (Rom. 5:8) | _____ _____ _____ _____ |
| Therefore be imitators of God | _____ |

as dear children. And walk in
love, as Christ also has loved
us and given Himself for us, an
offering and a sacrifice to God
for a sweet-smelling aroma.
(Eph. 5:1–2)

---------------------------------
---------------------------------
---------------------------------
---------------------------------
---------------------------------
---------------------------------

These things I command you,
that you love one another.
(John 15:17)

---------------------------------
---------------------------------
---------------------------------

• *In what ways are you feeling challenged in your spirit?*

_____

_____

## A Much-Needed Gift in the Church

In any body of believers, there are likely to be more people who feel they have a gift of mercy than any other ministry gift—and I believe that is healthy for the church. If the church is truly to be a "family," then love, kindness, tenderness, forgiveness, and mercy must be freely flowing. Any body of believers that is characterized by mercy is going to be a healthy body of believers. Those who show mercy certainly are going to provide a spiritually healthful and a practically helpful balance to those who have other ministry gifts.

Very often God puts us into marriage unions and business partnerships with those who have a "balancing" gift to the one we have. The gift of mercy is certainly a gift that balances several of the other gifts. It is the supreme balance for the gift of prophecy. In situations in which prophets may wound with their sharp denunciation of evil and their strong call to righteousness, the person with a gift of mercy is needed to "bandage" the wounded.

When any of us are being tempted, tried, or are undergoing

a difficult period, we long for those who will show mercy to us. We need the tenderness and love they show.

- *What new insights do you have into the gift of mercy?*

  _____

  _____

- *In what ways are you feeling challenged in your spirit?*

  _____

  _____

• *In what ways are you feeling challenged in your spirit?*

_____

_____

## Moving Beyond Your Own Ministry Gift

A faithfulness to one's own motivational gift does not mean on occasion that we cannot step into other ministry roles. For example, let us assume that people are required to direct the parking for a church so that parking is orderly and the church services can begin promptly. Helping to park cars is a ministry that is often undertaken joyfully and successfully by those who have the motivational gift of service. Let us further assume, however, that your particular gift is the gift of exhortation. Helping with the parking lot is not a ministry to which you would gravitate, choose, or in which you would find satisfaction week after week. But on any given Sunday, should there be a lack of people to assist with this ministry, you certainly would be capable of assisting in this ministry and be able to do so with success.

The Holy Spirit will help each of us to function outside of our innate motivational gift *if the need arises*. On the whole, however, a person is going to find the greatest satisfaction, fulfillment, and success when he or she operates within his or her motivational gift.

To say to another person, "Oh, I can't help you with that urgent need right now—that isn't my ministry gift" would be both presumptuous and prideful. When crises arise, the Holy Spirit's grace can help any believer to respond effectively as long as the person is willing to be used and empowered by the Spirit.

If you are gifted as a teacher, however, it would be wise for you to say, "Oh, yes, I can teach Sunday school this year," and unwise for you to say, "Yes, I'll take on the responsibilities of organizing the lay ministry to those who are homebound or in nursing homes." The person gifted in teaching will find fulfillment as a teacher, and although he or she may be capable of leading the nursing-home ministry, the person will *not* find that work fulfilling, and he will not be as effective or satisfied in the role as a person who truly is gifted in organization.

Using this same example, we must also recognize that for a person gifted as a teacher to *decline* a teaching opportunity out of rebellion, false humility, or misplaced priorities would be an act of disobedience to the Lord. The Lord has given us our motivational gifts for us to *use* them, and He will always present to us ample opportunities for us to use them so that we might grow in them and bless others. Be open to the ways in which the Holy Spirit may lead you into opportunities to use your gifts. Even though you may be a bit fearful or concerned about how well you may do in the ministry role presented to you—which is a natural response even if you are gifted in a particular area—say yes to the Lord and then trust the Holy Spirit to help you use your gift to the best of your ability.

## What the Word Says

To obey is better than sacrifice. (1 Sam. 15:22)

All things are lawful for me, but not all things are helpful; all things are lawful for me, but not all things edify. Let no one seek his own, but each one the other's well-being. (1 Cor. 10:23–24)

By the grace of God I am what I am, and His grace toward me was not in vain; but I labored more abundantly . . . yet not I, but the grace of God which was with me. (1 Cor. 15:10)

## What the Word Says to Me

-------------------------------
-------------------------------

-------------------------------
-------------------------------
-------------------------------
-------------------------------
-------------------------------
-------------------------------

-------------------------------
-------------------------------
-------------------------------
-------------------------------
-------------------------------
-------------------------------

# Developing Your Motivational Gift • 103

Let us therefore come boldly
to the throne of grace, that we
may obtain mercy and find
grace to help in time of need.
(Heb. 4:16)

- *In what ways are you feeling challenged in your spirit?*

## What About Manifesting the "Gifts of the Spirit"?

Just as we are to manifest the ministry of Jesus Christ to the world, believers in Christ should bear the likeness of the Holy Spirit into the world. The "fruit" of the Spirit is to become our character as we employ our ministry gifts (see Gal. 5:22–23). Furthermore, we should be willing at all times to manifest *any and all* of the spiritual gifts of the Holy Spirit *should He desire to use us for His ministry purposes.*

We are to be clean and pure vessels through which the Holy Spirit might pour His power, love, wisdom, and assistance. The spiritual gifts often called the "gifts of the Spirit"—such as those identified in 1 Corinthians 12:8–10—are gifts that belong to the Holy Spirit and are identified by the apostle Paul as being given by the Holy Spirit. They are aspects of the Holy Spirit's own power that He imparts to believers on occasion in order for the believer to minister more effectively to others. In the operation of these spiritual gifts, it is the Holy Spirit that provides the motivation or inspiration to the believer to act in a specific way at a specific time and for a specific purpose. As the believer is obedient to the Holy Spirit and allows the Holy Spirit to work in him and through him, the believer then acts *as Jesus would act* toward meeting the need in another person's life.

These spiritual gifts of the Holy Spirit are not resident in the believer, but are resident in the Spirit. They are not for the benefit of the believer through whom they function; they are for the benefit of another person who is experiencing need or trouble. They should bring no glory to the person who manifests them; all praise and honor should be given to the Holy Spirit from whom they flow.

The difference between these spiritual gifts and the motivational gifts is this: the spiritual gifts in 1 Corinthians 12:8–10 are resident in the Holy Spirit and they operate totally at the will of the Spirit. The motivational gifts are resident in us— imparted to us on a permanent basis by the Holy Spirit at the time of our acceptance of Jesus Christ as Savior, and they are never recalled from our lives. They operate to a great extent as we will them to operate—in other words, as we develop them and choose to use them.

- *What new insights do you have into the difference between the operation of the ministry gift resident in you as a believer and the operation of the gifts resident in the Holy Spirit?*

_____

_____

| What the Word Says | What the Word Says to Me |
|---|---|
| The one and the same Spirit works all these things, distributing to each one individually as He wills. (1 Cor. 12:11) | _____ _____ _____ _____ |
| Now God has set the members, each one of them, in the body just as He pleased. And if they were all one member, where would the body be? (1 Cor. 12:18–19) | _____ _____ _____ _____ _____ _____ |

## Developing Your Spiritual Gifts

The development of your spiritual gifts begins with an act of faith in the Lord Jesus Christ that He can and will work through you. The automatic outpouring of faith is a tangible form of ministry to others. If we truly believe what we say we believe about Jesus Christ, then our belief will *compel* us to act. We cannot *not* act. We must be obedient to what we know is true about God the Father, Jesus Christ, and the work of the Holy Spirit. As James wrote, "Be doers of the word, and not hearers only" (James 1:22).

As we turn from sin and disobedience, and choose to believe in Jesus Christ, trust God in all things, and obey God's commandments and the leading of the Holy Spirit, we are prepared and made "ready" for service. The Holy Spirit who indwells you as a believer will prepare you for ministry, direct you to ministry, and empower you for ministry.

| What the Word Says | What the Word Says to Me |
|---|---|
| If anyone cleanses himself . . . he will be a vessel for honor, sanctified and useful for the Master, prepared for every good work. (2 Tim. 2:21) | _____ |
| Hold fast the pattern of sound words which you have heard from me, in faith and love which are in Christ Jesus. That good thing which was committed to you, keep by the Holy Spirit who dwells in us. (2 Tim. 1:13–14) | _____ |

• *In your life, have you found that at times you believe so strongly about something that you must act?*

_____

_____

• *Have you had an experience in which you felt that the Holy Spirit was working through you to help others?*

_____

_____

Once we have a full understanding that Jesus Christ can and does work in us and through us—and that He desires to do so continually by the power of the Holy Spirit—we are called to develop our ministry gift in these four ways:

1. *We must choose to walk in the Holy Spirit daily.* We must examine our own lives, repent of our own willful pride in choosing to do things our way, and intentionally yield control of our lives to the Holy Spirit. We must give God permission to work in us and through us. We must ask for the help and guidance of the Holy Spirit on a daily basis. We must be sensitive at all times to the opportunities that the Holy Spirit is putting in our path.

## What the Word Says

As you therefore have received Christ Jesus the Lord, so walk in Him, rooted and built up in Him and established in the faith. (Col. 2:6–7)

I say then: Walk in the Spirit, and you shall not fulfill the lust of the flesh. (Gal. 5:16)

## What the Word Says to Me

-----------------------------

-----------------------------

-----------------------------

-----------------------------

-----------------------------

-----------------------------

-----------------------------

-----------------------------

• *Identify an experience you have had when you truly knew you were "walking in the Spirit."*

_____

_____

2. *We must learn all we can about the characteristics of our particular ministry gift.* Our prayer should continually be, "Lord, help me to understand this precious gift that You have given me and to know how best to develop it and use it." The best source for learning about your particular motivational gift is always going to be the Word of God. Study the lives of those who seem to embody your particular ministry gift. Read everything that Jesus had to say about your gift. Read what Paul, John, and others in the New Testament wrote about the employment of your gift. Grow in your understanding of *how* God intends for you to use your gift.

| What the Word Says | What the Word Says to Me |
|---|---|
| All Scripture is given by inspiration of God, and is profitable for doctrine, for reproof, for correction, for instruction in righteousness, that the man of God may be complete, thoroughly equipped for every good work. (2 Tim. 3:16–17) | ---------------------------- <br> ---------------------------- <br> ---------------------------- <br> ---------------------------- <br> ---------------------------- <br> ---------------------------- <br> ---------------------------- |
| Be diligent to present yourself approved to God, a worker who does not need to be ashamed, rightly dividing the word of truth. (2 Tim. 2:15) | ---------------------------- <br> ---------------------------- <br> ---------------------------- <br> ---------------------------- <br> ---------------------------- |

3. *We must "major" on the development of our gift.* Focus on the gift you have been given. Run the race that the Lord has put before you with diligence, focus, and patience (see Heb. 12:1). Run with a single-minded goal of becoming an *expert contributor* of your ministry gift to the Body of Christ, with your eyes continually on the Lord and on His desires (see 1 Cor. 9:24). Put aside any distractions and refuse to take any detours.

Readjust your priorities so that your number-one emphasis is on the godly use of your ministry gift in as many situations and settings as possible—at home, on the job, in the community, and especially in your church.

## What the Word Says

Therefore we also, since we are surrounded by so great a cloud of witnesses, let us lay aside every weight, and the sin which so easily ensnares us, and let us run with endurance the race that is set before us, looking unto Jesus, the author and finisher of our faith. (Heb. 12:1–2)

Do you not know that those who run in a race all run, but one receives the prize? Run in such a way that you obtain it. And everyone who competes for the prize is temperate in all things. Now they do it to obtain a perishable crown, but we for an imperishable crown. (1 Cor. 9:24–25)

You must continue in the things which you have learned and been assured of. (2 Tim. 3:14)

I remind you to stir up the gift of God which is in you. (2 Tim. 1:6)

## What the Word Says to Me

**4.** *We must get involved in a ministry and use our gift to the best of our ability.* To a very great extent, motivational gifts are developed *through use.* Find a ministry about which you care deeply and offer your services (your gift). Get involved. The more you use your gift, the stronger you will become in it, the more effective you will be, and the greater benefit you will render to the Body of Christ. Paul wrote that we are to be like athletes in training when it comes to the exercise of our ministry gifts. A good training program requires regular and consistent effort. So, too, the employment of our motivational gifts. We must get involved and stay involved.

| What the Word Says | What the Word Says to Me |
|---|---|
| I will show you my faith by my works . . . Do you want to know, O foolish man, that faith without works is dead? . . . A man is justified by works, and not by faith only. (James 2:18, 20, 24) | ------------------------------ ------------------------------ ------------------------------ ------------------------------ ------------------------------ ------------------------------ ------------------------------ |
| But as God has distributed to each one, as the Lord has called each one, so let him walk. (1 Cor. 7:17) | ------------------------------ ------------------------------ ------------------------------ ------------------------------ |
| God has not given us a spirit of fear, but of power and of love and of a sound mind. (2 Tim. 1:7) | ------------------------------ ------------------------------ ------------------------------ ------------------------------ |

## Called to Bear Fruit

Jesus called His disciples to bear fruit—in fact, He said that we are to bear "much fruit" (see John 15:8). It is in our fruitfulness that Jesus Christ is expressed to the world and the Father is glorified.

As you trust God to work in your life, and as you learn to walk day by day in the Spirit, learning all you can about your ministry gift, focusing on its development, and using it at every opportunity . . . you *will* be fruitful. In fact, you cannot help but be fruitful! Why? Because it is the Holy Spirit who will be producing fruit in you and through you. He is the life that is surging through the Vine out into you as the "branch," and He will bear fruit. As Jesus taught,

> "Abide in Me, and I in you. As the branch cannot bear fruit of itself, unless it abides in the vine, neither can you, unless you abide in Me. I am the vine, you are the branches. He who abides in Me, and I in him, bears much fruit." (John 15:4–5)

Choose to abide in the Lord and be obedient to His call on your life—it is a call to minister in His name and for His glory. Be true to the motivational ministry gift He has given you.

- *What new insights do you have into the development and use of your motivational gift?*

  _____

  _____

- *In your life, can you identify opportunities for the use of your motivational gift?*

  _____

  _____

- *How do you feel about the opportunities that the Lord is putting before you to use your gifts for His glory?*

  _____

- *In what ways are you feeling challenged in your spirit?*

  _____

  _____

# CONCLUSION

# DO TRY THIS AT HOME!

The motivational gifts are designed to be used *together* to build up the church. One thing we must recognize is that the church is not a building or an organization—it is a living spiritual entity, a body composed of all people who believe in the Lord Jesus Christ as the Son of God and the Savior sent by God to reconcile mankind to Himself. Genuine "church members" are wherever you find believers in Jesus Christ. Sometimes that will be at work, or in the community as a whole. In many cases, you will find fellow believers—fellow "church members" in your own home!

Your ministry gift is to function in *all* settings, not merely when you are serving on a church committee or as a part of a church-sponsored program. Whatever your gift may be, find ways to employ it in love, humility, and peace to those around you, and in conjunction with other members of the Body of Christ.

You and your spouse are likely to have different ministry gifts. Openly acknowledge your differences and find ways in which you can work together, building up one another and your family rather than tearing one another down through criticism or competition.

You and your children may very well have different ministry

gifts. Again, openly acknowledge your gifts and seek ways of employing them in a harmonious way that builds up your family life. Members of an "extended family" may be those who supply the ministry gifts that are missing from your immediate family.

The godly use of our ministry gifts is intended to bring glory to God. Make that your goal always. Exercise your ministry gift as you believe the Lord Jesus Christ would manifest your particular gift—seek to do what He would do and to say what He would say. And always, use your ministry gift with the fullness of the character of the Holy Spirit: "love, joy, peace, longsuffering, kindness, goodness, faithfulness, gentleness, and self-control" (Gal. 5:22–23). If you use your gift while manifesting the true character of our Lord, you *will* be a blessing to others . . . and you will reap the Lord's rewards and blessings in return.

—————— *NOTES* ——————